THE REV

Memoirs of Montreal's Old Brewery Mission

by

The Reverend Canon Bill McCarthy

Canadian Cataloguing in Publication Data

McCarthy, Bill, 1931-

ISBN 1-895854-61-X

1. McCarthy, Bill, 1931- . 2. Old Brewery Mission. 3. Homeless persons - Services for - Quebec (Province) - Montréal. 4. Church work with the homeless - Quebec (Province) - Montréal. 5. Church of England - Quebec (Province) - Montréal - Clergy - Biography. I. Hughson, Janet. II. Title.

BX5620.M224A3 1996   283',092   C96-940283-X

You may request our current catalogue by sending
your name and address to:

Robert Davies Publishing,
P.O. Box 702, Outremont, Québec, Canada H2V 4N6

Or see our electronic catalogue on the Internet at
http://www.rdp.com

THE REV

Memoirs of Montreal's Old Brewery Mission

By The Reverend Canon Bill McCarthy

Edited by Janet Hughson

Robert Davies Publishing   Montreal   1996

Text by The Reverend Canon Bill McCarthy
Edited by Janet Hughson
Cartoons by Aislin
Photographs by Earle McCarthy,
except where otherwise indicated
Book design and production by Mary Hughson

This book may be ordered in Canada from
General Distribution Services:
☎ 1-800-387-0141 / 1-800-387-0172   FAX: 1-416-445-5967

In the U.S.A. toll free 1-800-805-1083
or from the publisher, toll free across North America
1-800-481-2440, FAX: 514-481-9973

Contents

Introduction

Bill was always a tough nut; but then, he had to be.

During his time at the Old Brewery Mission, Reverend William McCarthy came to be known in and around Montreal simply as "The Rev" – or *"Le Rév"* in the French press.

Having grown up in a scrappy Montreal neighborhood known as Mile End, an 18 year old Bill McCarthy enlisted in the infantry to serve for two years in the Korean War. (Later, he would set up the Korean War Veteran's Association.)

Back in Montreal, Bill graduated from McGill's Diocesan College and, after being ordained in 1960, served at St. Barnabas Anglican Church in Roxboro,.where he built the parish up from 60 families to 600 within three years. In 1963, McCarthy was asked to take over at the OBM which had existed at various downtown locations since 1889. Over the next 30 years, Bill piloted the mission through its most tumultuous period.

Named Montreal's Irishman of the Year in 1984, McCarthy's valuable work was recognized by numerous organizations, culminating in his being named to The Order of Canada in 1985.

Shortly before his well-earned retirement in 1993, McCarthy lost one leg to diabetes and then, shortly thereafter, lost the second. To get beyond the experience, Bill began to write, hunkered down in a wheelchair using a beat-up computer that had been scrounged for him somewhere.

One hundred thousand words later, The Rev had a collection of memoirs of his experiences with an array of characters. McCarthy not being a writer by trade, had the meat for a book-that clearly required some careful work. In stepped Janet Hughson who knew that in order to retain The Rev's original flavor, she'd have to concoct a home-made stew, not filet mignon ("I hope she keeps the Irish," Bill had said). And that Janet did. Having read McCarthy's original manuscript, I know that she has done an exceptional job of editing this book.

Welcome to the world of the unfortunate where few have the courage to tread, trusting that the likes of "The Rev" will do it for them.

Terry Mosher (Aislin)
Montreal

Dedication

This book is dedicated to all those individuals who persevered and shared with me during my thirty years at the mission. This includes the thousands of donors and supporters who helped make it all possible and those members of the staff who gave so much of themselves. I am very proud of them all.

I also dedicate this book to my wife Colette and son Earle who cheerfully supported a man always on the run, busy with a special vocation.
Finally, to the three lovely people who made this dream of a book possible, Janet Hughson, Mary Hughson and Terry Mosher.

Bill McCarthy
February 14, 1996

Two residents of the OBM   *John Mahoney, The Gazette*

A Labour of Love

I am only one,
but I am one.

I cannot do everything,
but I can do something.

What I can do, I ought to do
and what I ought to do,
by the grace of God I will do.

The Rev. Canon Farrar

Trying to put your life's work into words is much like trying
to relive your life and I have learned to accept that yesterday is
gone. So why bother? Why write a book? Maybe the answer to
that is as simple — and as complicated — as I am. But I believe
both in the brotherhood of man and that as a priest, I have an

obligation to help people.

Some very significant things have happened over the life of the Old Brewery Mission (OBM). Unless they are recorded, they may well be glossed over and forgotten in the next few years. A Mission is more than opening the doors at supper time and turning the men out after breakfast. That just isn't good enough. A mission must be compassionate, caring, hospitable and encouraging. People who came to the Mission were always treated as human beings. The very few who were turned away had to have been very, very bad. In the late 1980's, the City of Montreal and the Government of Quebec selected the Old Brewery Mission as the agency best suited to meet the needs of the homeless and needy of Montreal. Those standards have got to be kept up.

For those of us serving at the Mission, sacrifices of family time were part of the commitment we made. There were never enough hours in the days and weeks. I would often forget to pick up the telephone until the last minute to say "Sorry, I won't be home for supper tonight" or "There's a meeting and I have to go because they want me to accept a cheque for the Mission." Fortunately I was blessed to be married to a very special person, someone understanding and devoted, who did not merely stand by and pray, but dedicated thousands of unpaid hours of work to the Mission and its summer camp, as an act of love. Time and again, Colette Asselin McCarthy also forced me to think in new ways about situations we faced which seemed impossible, unmanageable or just wild. We would talk things over and I would usually say: "Show me why I should do it." Colette would calmly answer: "Why not?" Not being able to come up with a good reason "why not" was often a sign we should try something new. It would invariably work out.

The strength and happiness of our home made life at the Mission tolerable even if it was tough. Whenever I felt a burn-out coming on, I would retreat into a weekend's — or a week's — binge of reading fiction: espionage, detective stories or the current best sellers. Putting aside the woes of mission life for a few days gave me back my strength and I could return to action after the brief R & R.

Chapter One

Some people dislike travel. I loved to drive, consistently running up seventy-five to a hundred thousand miles a year in a variety of cars and trucks. The time driving, away from the infernal telephone and people barging in to ask you to stop whatever you were doing and settle something, was seldom wasted. I used it as prayer time. With my car as my place of meditation, and those stretches of highway in front of me, I found strength and inspiration each day.

During a recent American college football pre-game show, the sportscaster paused in his praise of the talents of the Auburn home team to talk to the visiting Notre Dame coach. "Lou Holtz," he said, "what do you think of your chances here today? This glorious football team has close to one hundred thousand fans cheering them on to victory. And what about this terrible rain storm? How are you going to cope with all that?"

The old coach looked at the announcer, smiled and said, "It's not my job to worry about who we play or where we play, nor is it my job to worry about what kind of weather we play in. My job is how we play. Have a nice day." And with that, he trotted onto the playing field. Notre Dame won the game.

"How you play" is in many ways what life is all about. The coach had it right: we cannot always pick our playing field. However, whether it's the high altar in the Cathedral, the work bench, office or the battlefield, we are all called upon to be worthy of our vocations.

During my youth I was inspired by some pretty dedicated and outstanding clergy. When I hear of all the turmoil and pain that many people have had with unfaithful and perverted clergy, I can look back gratefully on a rich and wonderful parish life. A succession of good parish priests had a big impact upon me: the Rev. Fred Morris (later Archdeacon), the Rev. Arthur Coleman, later Dean of Quebec, the Rev. Gordon Addie, war hero and later Canon, and finally my mentor-tormentor and good friend, the Rev. Roland Bodger. All helped guide me into full-time service. Roland Bodger's sermons in particular have stuck with me and I think quite often of a poem he once quoted:

THE OLD BREWERY MISSION

" I would rather see a sermon
than hear one any day.
I would rather someone lead me
than to merely point the way..."

That is what I believe my work at the Old Brewery Mission was all about: living out my sermons, helping people along the way.

There was never any question as to how, what or who motivated the work of the Mission. It was always a Christian mission serving the children of God regardless of race, religion or colour. Our Blessed Lord could, would and did sustain it. I saw a great number of very ill people pass through the doors of the Old Brewery Mission during my 30 years (1963 to 1993) there. But I also saw a lot of individual miracles of one sort or another and I firmly believe they were sent to help us along the road of life.

There are hundreds of incidents — births, deaths, laughter and tears — that I shall always remember; stories of people who lived or worked at the Mission and their families. Perhaps that was the key: we were like family at the Mission for thirty years. People who worked there were family and we shared and fought like families. Maybe we were too closely intertwined with each other, but it helped make the Mission what it was.

With a very few exceptions, the names used in this brief account are invented to protect the families involved and to uphold the trust that has always existed between the men and the Mission.

As the old gospel singer Edward MacHugh used to sing nightly on the radio when I was a boy, "If I have wounded any soul today, Dear Lord forgive."

Reverend Canon Bill McCarthy

Miss Mina E. Douglas & Mrs. Frank D. Adams,
co-founders of Montreal's Old Brewery Mission

The Beginnings of The Old Brewery Mission

What an unusual name for an organization dedicated to helping the poor and needy of the greater Montreal area! People often think the Mission must have been started and run by the Molson family. In fact, although Senator Molson and his family do support the Mission and have been very faithful over the years, the distinction of founding the Mission in the 1880's belongs to two very persuasive ladies from a downtown church which was then known as the Dominion Square Methodist Church.

Being situated in the core of the city, the church had needy people coming every day and asking for something to eat or help in finding a place to sleep. Miss Mina Douglas and Miss Eva Findlay were very dedicated Christian women who persisted in their efforts to get the church involved in a soup kitchen for the poor men who came looking for something to eat. These two ladies not only had a lot of spunk, but they also had more than a little clout: Miss Douglas was a member of the Douglas family after whom the Douglas Hospital and Dominion Douglas Church were named and Miss Findlay later married Dean Adams of McGill University.

The soup kitchen was duly opened and within a month, the ladies were shocked to learn that many of the men were sleeping outside in porches or wagons during the winter.

At a church board meeting, they convinced the men of the Church to look for sleeping quarters for the men and in due course, the committee located an abandoned building which had once housed the Williams Brewery. When it opened as a men's shelter, the men used to say, "I'm going to the old brewery." Because it was sponsored by the Church, it was naturally a mission, so eventually the name Old Brewery Mission (or OBM) came into common usage.

During the late 1940's and early 1950's, there was a rash of organizational name changes; for example, the Verdun Protestant Hospital became the Douglas, and so on. However, it was decided that the Old Brewery Mission was known by that name across the country and men in need would recognize it. No changes were made.

Over the next seventy-five years, the Mission would move seven times, each time finding new quarters with great difficulty; society wanted nothing to do with the men who frequented the Mission. In 1925, when union among the Presbyterian, Congregational and Methodist Churches took place, the number of church buildings required dropped considerably. On the corner of Delisle and Canning Streets, there was an abandoned church for sale. The Old Brewery Mission bought and refurbished it, but a group of citizens led by a local minister managed to keep them out in the end. The CNR then rented the Mission a property temporarily until the Mission moved to 529 Inspector Street.

During those first seventy-five years, there were four wars in which young Canadian men fought in foreign lands. The country also struggled through the Depression and numerous recessions. The Mission remained open through it all. Conservative estimates place the number of beds filled at 250,000 and the number of meals served at 500,000.

The following twenty-five years brought enormous change. One of the things we had to deal with was a challenge to the organization's name by l'Office de la langue française. I must admit that the person handling the complaint was very gracious when I noted that the word "brasserie" today means drinking establishment, not a brewery and that "mission" is in any case the same in both languages. We came to a verbal agreement that henceforward, signs in front of the building would read "Mission Old Brewery Mission". We were open to everyone and in fact, there was no Francophone mission at that time, la Maison du Père not having been opened.

More importantly, we were dealing with a doubling and even tripling of the demand in services. Merely providing food and shelter was not going to be enough in the new era. It was time to completely rethink how we brought our mission to those in need.

The Old
Brewery Mission,
then and now

Chapter Three

The OBM and the Changing Social Services Landscape

The City of Montreal's Executive Committee used to make tours of inspection of the various wards of the city. Two or three busloads of advisors, planners and works department people did the rounds. Our St. Laurent Boulevard buildings, one of four stories and the other of three, both fronting on The Main, eventually came under scrutiny. One day the grand tour began at St. Antoine and St. Laurent. There, in a state of abject poverty, was the back end of the Old Brewery Mission, store windows boarded up and posters all over the place. Guess what? We had building inspectors swarming over us for months after. I let the Board of Directors know what was happening but at first they thought it was just another attempt on my part to complete the building project started in 1966. When a letter threatening legal action came, everyone realized it was really serious. By not completing the original project in 1967, we avoided spending $150,000; now the renovations were going to cost us $2,000,000.

I had managed to get the idea across to the City that we would like to do this project as part of our 100th anniversary celebrations and could probably raise the money then. The city inspector told me there were all kinds of grants that would provide up to 80% financing. We were told we absolutely had to find someone who knew the inner workings of the grant system if we wanted to get the project on its way.

As the project developed, each and every item was reviewed by the City, our architect and ourselves. Fortunately the fellow handling the file in the City of Montreal Planning Department knew the Mission well; he was a reformed alcoholic who fought our case as far as he could. When he could make no further progress, he called. "Mr. McCarthy," he said, "you will need some heavy help to get a break on the amount of the grant."

Who else was there to call but our building chairman and the original Mr. Fixit, Roger Beaulieu?

Sometime later that same week I received a phone call from a somewhat aggrieved City employee. "You didn't tell me the President of the Vieux Port de Montréal was on your Board of Directors." (Roger Beaulieu was Vice-President of the Mission.)

I wouldn't want to get into cause and effect, but we got a grant of $1,200,000 and were more than halfway home. On the other side of my face was just as big a grin because we were also able to tap into the Prime Minister's $300 million promise of support a couple of months before that budget was cut.

"Well sir," said the City employee, "now that you have approval of the grant, where will you be operating from during the construction?"

"We will get an office on the corner of University and Dorchester from our President, who owns the building", said I, with a grin like the cat that swallowed the canary.

"Mr. McCarthy, René Lévesque Boulevard, please." (The City of Montreal had just changed the name of Dorchester Boulevard to that of the late Premier of Quebec and I couldn't resist needling them.)

He wanted to know where the men would go during construction and I advised him that we would take them up to our summer camp. He was horrified. "Oh, no! The City can't permit that. The Salvation Army is under construction and now the Mission, too. You just can't close." So the journey to Sanguinet Street and Dernier Recours began.

~

Dernier Recours Montréal (DRM)

First I should back up and explain how Dernier Recours Montréal came to be.

It seemed at one time as if all the individual groups working in the field of social assistance insisted that their particular way of tackling the problems was the only way. It was a case of: *Just give us a cheque and let us get on with the job*. To its credit, the City of Montreal decided to see just exactly what was really needed in the way of assistance and during the Year of the Homeless, came up with a plan to study the issue. Oh, great!, I thought, just what we need — another study. Why can't the Government do something without a vested interest study? However it's true that you often can't see the forest for the trees. Those of us working in the field had had little opportunity to look at alternatives to the way we had traditionally provided services and certainly — heaven forbid — to undertake studies. It was a luxury we just couldn't afford. Mayor Jean Doré insisted that before we put big dollars into anything, we had to know what we were getting into. Although I hated the idea passionately, I learned over the following two years or so just what good research and planning could do for us.

The City Council did its homework and organized a series of hearings and very shortly thereafter, the City announced the opening of a referral service called Dernier Recours Montréal (DRM), dubbed Last Chance Hostel in English. What a joke it seemed to many of us: all the hostels were full — to whom were they going to refer these people in need of shelter?

In those early days, we weren't really aware of who was organizing this project and were not that keen to find out about it. However, James McGregor (Secretary to the City's Executive Committee Chairman) reminded me that unless we cooperated and supported the new DRM project, we would appear to be against progress. Most existing agencies working with the homeless were then co-opted to serve on the Board of Directors of Dernier Recours and that is how we began to share in this new endeavour.

Often it is just the simple things that bring credibility to an effort. Mayor Doré showed up at the hearings and listened carefully to the questions that were asked. People began to believe something was actually in the air. The machinery was set in motion and municipal government agencies geared up to support the project. The City Housing Corporation (SDHM) made various buildings available and became deeply involved in the problems of the homeless in general. Basically Mayor Doré, John Gardiner (Chairman of the Executive Committee) and his successor, Lea Cousineau, were exactly the supporters we needed to make sense out of the new program.

Naturally merchants and citizens alike were concerned: anywhere but not in my district. At one meeting with the merchants of St. Catherine Street, Madame Cousineau said we were going to go ahead with a 29-bed hostel for men and women on St. Hubert Street and would have regular meetings with the merchants to discuss any problems. No problems, no meetings. None were needed.

Now that I have withdrawn from active participation in the work among the homeless and destitute of Montreal, I honestly think that the only other time major government personalities got really involved in alleviating human suffering was back during the days of the plague on Montreal's waterfront during the 19th century. At that time, many citizens, including a Mayor of Montreal, actually died helping the poor immigrants placed in isolation in the waterfront sheds. While I may be suspected of over-dramatizing, I stand by the judgment: not one City of Montreal department head was left untouched by this new fight on behalf of the homeless. A review of the newspapers and film clips of the goings-on at Dernier Recours will show you city councillors and politicians leading one fight or the other, actually mixing in with and helping people! And who ever heard of a Minister of Health and Welfare actually getting involved with the homeless and destitute people of the province?

~

Opening the country's eyes

The fact that Mayor Doré had placed two of the most efficient scroungers of any city department at the helm of Dernier Recours (Director Marie Audet and Assistant Director André Jacob) really got things off on the right foot. At the point where we were ready to start renovations at the Mission and needed temporary quarters, Marie Audet suggested that we could probably use an upper floor in the school where Dernier Recours was located in Sanguinet Street. After a short discussion, we signed a $1 lease and the saga was launched.

Before moving into the temporary quarters in the old Alexandria School on Sanguinet Street, we had to install toilets, showers and sinks. The population of the Mission had increased dramatically. With close to 100 hundred men up north in Camp Chapleau, we also operated l25 to 150 beds on Sanguinet Street, close to doubling our usual capacity under very trying conditions.

Then too, at Marie Audet's insistence and for the first time in my memory, we admitted women to a special dormitory. One day while the men were painting the offices, there was loud laughter from all the painters. They were witnessing a group sex party in a doorway right across the street! Fortunately we never had that problem inside the building; everyone knew that retribution would be sure and swift.

Montrealers began to really see for the first time what it was like to be living on the street downtown. Ordinary missions like ours had been doing this kind of work for a hundred years and had become largely invisible; just a normal part of the social structure. It was a shock to society to actually see on television the human tragedies that were being enacted on St. Catherine and Sanguinet Streets day and night.

There was no doubt from the outset that we would have problems in this most volatile area of the city, but when you get squads of police cars screeching to a stop in front of your building five to ten times daily, you begin to think you are in some kind of a war zone. The police always arrived in no less than three cruisers with two constables in each car. That speaks for itself.

DRM had a policy that anyone and everyone were to be accepted. We in turn had agreed to accept people up until midnight and even later if they were quiet. We found ourselves doing things that we never would have done before. Our own flexibility amazed us! Marie Audet became quite a spokesperson for the homeless and in doing so became a target for the conventional agencies. Article after article plus horrific pictures in the newspapers and exposes on television brought the problem directly to the general public. It was only then that people began to realize that we really did have a serious problem in Montreal. I could have talked until I was blue in the face and people would have said "Nice talking to you, Father" and ignored me. Now the living proof was there for all to see and it wasn't nice.

Marie did her job well and she was ably supported by André Jacob in trying to deal with the pressures generated by infighting and dealing with the opposition party, the constituents, merchant associations and taxpayers. Accounts payable began to pile up until eventually they had to request a bail-out. Pressure was placed on provincial authorities for financial help and they really came through, despite awesome odds and budget difficulties.

Marie and André fought to the bitter end of Dernier Recours. Labour strife was the official reason for its demise. I was on the Board of Directors at the time and although I must agree that labour problems were the nail in the coffin, it went far deeper than that. Intense pressure from the St. Catherine Street merchants, hypocrisy from the CLSC Centre-Ville, jealousy on the part of the Réseau d'aide and the "show" in the street outside DRM, with the strikers from DRM as supporting actors, turned Marie's best resource — the media — against her. The Centre was doomed. Somebody pulled the plug. The workers thought they could serve the needy in front of the television cameras, but the big decision was made at a much higher level and they all lost their jobs.

Nonetheless, the countless research projects and studies Marie and André had compiled began to pay off. A new house for 15 women and 14 men was opened on St. Hubert Street, right behind the bus terminal. Following close behind was a new unit for 75 transients on Hochelaga Street, in the east end of the city. And finally, a special 35 beds are held at the Old Brewery Mission for transients. The Social Affairs Department of the Gouvernement du Québec subsidizes this program for $400,000 each year — it would cost close to double that amount to have another group run these houses.

At the Mission, we had already put in place new administrative systems and controls which were flexible enough to adapt to the needs of this new program. The OBM's track record was a major factor in getting the grants approved. Mr. Prud'homme, special assistant to the Deputy Minister of Social Affairs, was a strong guiding light for us. One day he regretfully announced that he could only guarantee money for emergency shelter — nothing for food.

I told him not to worry. "We will find a way to provide something to eat before they go to bed and something to eat before they go out on the streets in the morning. That's always been Mission policy and I see no reason for us not to be able to contribute to this project in a tangible way." He promised that somehow he would get us extra money the next year — and he did.

Superstar Céline Dion to transport guests to her wedding by bus.

Cruisin'...

Good timing is always critical to the success of these endeavours; Marie Audet was an excellent networker and very astute about taking advantage of any situation that presented itself.

For example, Marie had a friend with a very good position at Hydro Quebec. As the story goes, Marie and her friend were at a Hydro social event one evening and she was introduced to someone who offered her some used clothing for homeless and destitute people: old Hydro uniforms, shirts, boots, nylon parkas and so on. They were given to her on the condition that we were to remove all the Hydro Quebec crests and insignia, which we agreed to do. Within a week, the Chief of Hydro

Quebec Security was back with a group of their police and con-
fiscated every piece of the old Hydro clothing they could find
at the Mission!

Apparently what had happened was that one of the men
assigned to remove the crests found a complete uniform that fit
him like a glove. He shined his shoes, went up the street to
Hydro headquarters and demanded his old job back. Did that
door ever slam fast! When he learned about this escapade,
Rock Carignan, my assistant director, shook with anger; by his
foolishness, that man had as good as stolen good clothing off
the backs of people who really needed it. Well, we tried.

One day I talked to Marie about my dream of having a bus to
make regular runs during bad weather to literally rescue men off
the streets. The trouble was, getting a bus was one thing and
operating it was another. A few speeches to service clubs and
Masonic Lodges and the skilled scroungers at the Mission could
come up with a old school bus in working order, but how were
we going to pay a driver and cover repairs and gas? That was
when Marie's well-trained public service mind came into play.

"Bill," she said, "make an estimate of how much it will cost
you to run the bus. Then include those figures in your budget
as transportation costs when you make the presentation for the
new satellites you will be operating for the Government."

The City of Montreal had its back against the wall because
the local merchants were screaming to get the homeless
vagrants out of their district, hence the interest in decentraliz-
ing services for the homeless. The Old Brewery Mission was
being asked to operate these facilities because of our effective
operations and independence from government money over the
past hundred years.

On Marie's advice, the calculations were made and submitted.
The Government of Quebec had just announced deep budget
cuts and no more money was to be found; the best they could
do was to put up $400,000 for sleeping accommodations. We'd
have to find ways to feed and transport them. We counter-
offered, undertaking to supply the food if the City of Montreal
would come up with transport. The City didn't appreciate
being backed into a corner one bit, but after they got bids from

commuter and school bus companies, they realized our estimates were a third of what they would be charged by private
contractors.

And so our dream came true: the City included transportation
in the budget. We ought to say "Thank you!" to John Bradley
of the Montreal Housing Society (SDHM) for his support
throughout.

My son Earle established the bus route and pick-up points
and went along on the evening runs. Earle was born the first
year I was at the Mission, so all the men knew him. One
evening there was a short film on television showing the bus in
action, with Earle leading the tour. When I saw the respect and
affection the men showed for him, I knew we had not made a
mistake in hiring him.

It wasn't long before the bus provided soup, coffee and sandwiches on board for the people they picked up. The bus was an
instant success and every hour during the evening it can be
seen wending its way along St. Catherine Street, stopping at
the various metro stations where people tend to take shelter
and driving them to the Mission. When Dernier Recours was
operating, it also made stops there to let off or take on people.

The bus became a light in the darkness; men and women in
need knew they could count on the bus coming. Around 8:30
each evening, the bus loads up with the first group of men who
will sleep in a satellite building about five miles from the city
centre. The men are transported back to the Mission before
eight each morning. The second group leaves around eleven
p.m. and a second run is made back each morning.

It was well into the third year when we had to make a decision:
repair costs and expenses were skyrocketing. My request to the
Board of Directors was tabled for further consideration. About
twenty-four hours later, one of the directors phoned me and said
"Bill, I wouldn't want the OBM to be found negligent if an accident was to happen with that old bus. How much will it cost?"

"Forty thousand," I said.

"If I were to buy it for you, could I pay for it over three years?"

Nearly falling through the floor, I quickly replied "No problem. That would be just wonderful." This very generous man

had from time to time made impossible dreams come true at the Mission and always anonymously, but this time we inscribed a plaque on the bus and were extremely happy to do so.

The agony of finding bus drivers with permits and then managing these hot-shots was another bag of problems. These guys thought they were pilots for Air Force One instead of the Old Brewery Mission bus. Some drivers took the bus home with them and never showed up the day after payday. Despite that, the bus project is real and meaningful and until the City cancels its agreement to bus people to the emergency houses, the expenses are covered.

Scripture tells us that "All things work together for good, for them that love and fear the Lord".

~

I shudder when I hear that all we need are administration whiz kids to handle the operation of a mission. It was a lot of little things that made the whole caring system work. People who didn't use to care seemed eventually to discover that so and so wasn't so bad after all. One by one people became aware of each other.

When we buried a fellow, I would somehow manage to take a few of the men I knew would miss their friend to the graveside committal. On the way home, we would usually stop at a classy brasserie, where we could have a hamburger and a bock of beer together in remembrance.

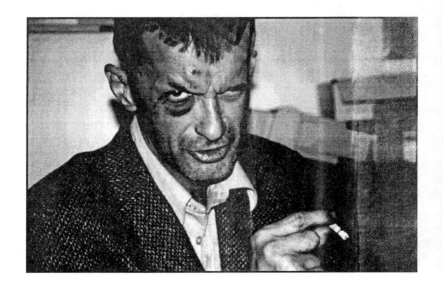

I Was Sick and You Cared For Me: Alcoholics Anonymous

The story of Alcoholics Anonymous (A.A.) is fascinating. It was founded by two Americans — Bill Wilson, a New York stockbroker, and Bob Smith, a doctor from Akron, Ohio. Wilson was the first of the two to stop drinking. However, it is significant that A.A. doesn't date its founding from that point. Instead, it recognizes June 10, 1935 as the true beginning of the organization, the day that Wilson helped Smith quit drinking for good; one drunk helping out another. They then formulated a set of steps that would help them and others to a new way of life. (I highly recommend The Big Book, published by A.A., and available in public libraries or through A.A. chapters.) Overcoming alcohol addiction requires enormous willpower and a strong desire to change one's way of life. A.A.

provides the tools and support necessary to help people on their return voyage to sobriety. What's the secret? Somebody helps you and you help somebody else.

In the very early years of A.A., "cold turkey" was the only accepted method of withdrawal, a truly brutal process. Now it is understood that the alcoholic requires long-term peer support and A.A. has so far proven to provide the best support structure. In some cases professional help is also required since alcohol is often used to camouflage a mental or physical illness. I was taught that alcoholism was a neurotic solution to a neurotic problem: take away the alcohol and you still have the problem. People who backslide are often unable to control their daily lives for medical or social reasons. When these underlying issues are dealt with, the A.A. program is a real success story and today most clinical detoxification centres include it in their therapy.

In my view, once someone is addicted, he no longer has any free will and can no longer tell the difference between right and wrong. Like any drug, the more alcohol is used, the more the body demands it. The attack on the central nervous system is vicious and the reduction of oxygen in the blood system, especially to the brain, has serious consequences. A.A. is to my mind a great alternative to the addiction: it demands a conversion to another way — sobriety, good friends, back-up support and a way of life that respects others. It takes a great deal of courage and self-discipline to start back up the ladder from the very bottom and as part of that healing process, to re-visit the living hell of all alcoholics, skid row. But that second look at skid row can play tricks on you, leave you feeling smug that you are not like those men and women and maybe give you just enough excuse to start drinking again. However, viewed with wisdom it can also remind you: "There but for the grace of God, go I".

~

My association with A. A. goes back to the early 1950's when the movement was just a youngster in Quebec. I was well aware of the problem of alcoholism, many of my old army pals from the Korean War having become very heavy drinkers. Hundreds of veterans of World War II with alcohol-related problems were already living at places like the Old Brewery Mission. Many more would soon follow. I started to see A.A. as an alternative for them.

When I was still at Saint Barnabas Church, Roxboro, an A.A. group wanted to get meetings started in the church basement. The church wardens confronted me, saying that the congregation wouldn't like it, wouldn't want "those kind of people" hanging around. Thirty-five years later, the group is still going strong.

At the time, I found encouragement in a story told by a Bishop from western Canada, recalling the early days of a group in his parish church. He decided that he was going to support them and attended every meeting during the winter months. But he never could figure out why not one of his parishioners was ever there. The following summer while out for an evening stroll, he passed the local United Church and there was a sign on the lawn which said "A. A. MEETING TONIGHT". So he decided to go in — and found that at least half of the people there were members of his parish!

~

The temptation to tell funny stories or tales of success about some of the men in the A.A. program is tremendous, but visitors at A.A. meetings are asked to maintain the anonymity of the people and I intend to honour that.

Over my thirty years at the Mission, I became very friendly with many area A.A. sponsors, trustees and workers, some of whom I met through Dr. Travis Dancey of Queen Mary Veterans' Hospital. One person who stands out is Barney, for all intents and purposes the Chief Executive Officer of the Leclerc Institute A.A. Group. He was an enormous man — six foot six and three hundred pounds if he was an ounce — who seemed to laugh all the time, whether with you or at you, you could never be sure. Anyway, most inmates didn't dare fool with him. Barney helped us in the Mission and later in founding and operating Saint Edward's house, which was the first English halfway house for ex-inmates in Montreal. He passed away very shortly after we got friendly with him, but we always remember his tremendous sense of humour and his intense desire to advance A.A.

Chapter Five

Another shining star was Doctor Geoff, one of the creators of Project Seven at Saint Anne's Veterans Hospital, which has over the years made some remarkable progress. Our particular interest in Project Seven was that we were able to get men from the Mission into the program if there was a vacancy at Senneville Lodge, where the program was run. The only conditions were that you had to be a veteran of one of the World Wars or Korea and that you had to be sober and have been abstinent for twenty-four hours to get in. (In the fifties, it was much more difficult — and expensive — to get booze on Sunday in Quebec, so Monday would be a day of suffering. Tuesday, after 48 hours of withdrawal, was admissions day.)

It was amazing to see men return from a good detoxification program like this one. If they went in during the summer, they came back all sun-tanned and filled out from the good food. The men we saw at the Mission were usually the ones who slipped from time to time and tried to get back into the project. The doctor was a no-nonsense guy, so when you were applying the second time, you really had to show a strong desire to improve. And improve some of them did. My old buddy from the Korean War, Jeff, has been sober for over twenty years, strictly adheres to a daily physical training program and stays away from the old gang, tavern or military. Gerry, another member of the program, married one of the nurses and is still a sponsor for the group in Saint Anne's Hospital today. Little Bobby never came back to the Mission after going through the program and I met him at an anniversary of Project Seven Group A.A., still sober after twenty-five years and still going to meetings.

One of my favourites was Jackie. Both he and his brother were Korean War veterans who used to drive me to complete distraction when they worked with us at the Mission. Doctor Geoff met his match when he allowed Jack to go into the program. Our friend was soft-spoken, kind, well-educated and brought-up and a true Jack of all trades. There was hardly anything he couldn't do, including getting whatever he wanted either by hard work or charm. I know I promised not to get into anyone's story, but Jack could charm anyone and he became a favourite at Saint Anne's and Senneville. Doctor Joe Csank was about the last remaining staff member of Project Seven and he vividly remembered Jack. While talking with a friend at the Saint Anne de Bellevue Legion at their annual Remembrance Dinner, Jack's name came up and we heard that he had moved to Vancouver to be with his brother before the latter's death.

Not long after that, Jack's wife (who had had to separate from him because of his abusive drinking) also died; Jack loved her very much but could never rebuild the bridge he had so badly burned. The friend expressed to Jack his hope that all these troubles would not make him start drinking again. Jack quickly replied, "If only you knew how low I went, you would understand why I will never touch a drink again. I never want to go back." He stayed sober over twenty years, worked in all kinds of jobs, including part-time at the local Legion as caretaker, janitor and occasionally, cook.

~

During the early 1960's, the men at the Mission had almost no contact with women and seemed a sexless sort of society. On the street, the men would never think of asking a woman for a handout: if the woman had made a fuss, they would have been in jail so fast their feet would never have hit the ground. At the Mission, there were two female secretaries who hardly had anything to do with the men, the Mission being basically out of bounds during the day. The French-speaking A.A. group was about to change all that.

In 1964, a Francophone from the Mission said that he was attending A.A. meetings elsewhere, but that he and a friend were interested in starting a group at the Mission. I said point blank that anything was better than what we had going for us and that I would appreciate their support. The Francophone meetings, as they are now called, were close to being revivalist, complete with lively and well-illustrated personal stories. But the other major attraction was that women came. The men at the Mission who decided to attend started to spruce up a bit, to clean up their act. They felt human again; women could and would talk to them. For years after, these men would return to the Mission and tell us how A.A. gave them a new start in life.

The devoted people who bring their message to the Mission week in and week out had a tough time getting the A.A. movement started at the OBM. The "in crowd" at the Mission (staff, cleaners, admission clerks and secretaries) were very vocal: "These people are not welcome. Who do they think they are? They're just a bunch of drunks and con artists. The program will never work here."

Some of the staff think they run the Mission, especially if the Director isn't around. Let loose, some of these people can undo a year's work in minutes on account of their jealousy of someone else getting ahead. Many Mission workers are on rehabilitation projects and the risk of such problems is always present.

Both French and English groups were subject to derision and sabotage. Sometimes it seemed that Satan himself took a hand in training the trouble-makers to drop a tray of dishes just when the poor guest speaker was telling his story for the first time. They would talk loudly, tell jokes, turn off the coffee machine, make sure the milk was sour or "disappear" the sugar. Donuts were mysteriously broken..."too fresh" apparently. Real little rays of sunshine.

However, the A.A. members were up to the challenge. The glorious thing was that almost every one of them, having hit a personal bottom, knew how to deal with all kinds of persecution and wouldn't be distracted from getting on with their program of self-rehabilitation. I well remember the time when the kitchen staff announced that the cafeteria, where the meetings are held, had to be closed at 10:30 a.m. so they could clean up for lunch. (The meeting had only got started at 9:30.) Now it happened that the sponsor of the English group had recently submitted to one of those gruelling "roasts" on the understanding that the proceeds from the evening's binge could go to the Old Brewery Mission. Well, after subjecting himself to that kind of sacrifice and severe self-discipline, our friend was in no mood to let the kitchen staff get away with their meanness. Having made a very large donation to the Mission, he spoke to the Director the next Monday morning and things began to improve dramatically. It was really remarkable to see the changes in the staff and the conditions of the hall for the next few months. However, it is important to realize that ill-founded suspicion is still very much alive and can do a lot of damage to people trying to recover from various kinds of addiction.

The program never was a rose garden. The groups had problems getting speakers, and they would shut down each summer for extended periods. After one very long summer, the group only re-opened late in October. While it was hard to see this happen, we had to stand aside and let things evolve on their own. The program often stuttered and restarted, but that is what alcoholism is all about, people with problems trying to work them out and sometimes falling and having to start all over again. It was that way with our group and probably evermore will be.

~

One cannot work with alcoholics without being at least aware of the A.A. program and its philosophy of living 24 hours at a time. As they say, "Unload the packsack of all your yesterdays and start with today and today only. You can build for tomorrow, but work on how you are going to get through today." There may not be thousands of success stories but enough to go around and more than enough for me to say "Try it — you might like it" to those who find that alcohol is beginning to be a problem in their lives.

After preaching that way of life for over thirty years it was easy for me to adapt it to my personal situation as I worked my way through a life-threatening diabetes problem. A.A. has changed the lives of hundreds of thousands of people and in old-fashioned Clark Street language, "Good on ya, A.A."

~

Suffering on Film

Several movies have been made in and around the Mission, but The Agony of Jimmy Quinlan stands out for its accurate portrayal of the agony of alcohol withdrawal. The producer was determined to get an honest story and Jimmy allowed his own name to be used as did most of the other skid row "actors". They were well paid to appear in the film and many celebrated their stardom with good quality alcohol for a change. Although the original producer eventually dropped out, a very sensitive writer/producer who knew the Mission and many of the men did an excellent job of pulling it all together.

This National Film Board production opens by exposing the flirtation with death that is panhandling on the Main. Bumming on the sidewalk is one thing; on a street with heavy traffic it's almost suicidal. Vagrants, alcoholics and drug abusers have paid the price of serious injury or death for this daring practice.

The story then moves on to Jimmy's life. Jimmy was not an illiterate, useless person. In fact he was well brought up and came from a very religious family. The reasons for his alcohol abuse were common ones: alcohol gave him power and friends and made it easier to convince himself that he had succeeded. In reality he had only succeeded in becoming the town drunk. Trying to sober up on your own or in your regular milieu is agony. The hounding and abuse of Jimmy portrayed in the film were usual Mission fare. Somehow the other men get the idea that this "Holy Joe" will put a stop to their own drinking unless they stop him. Unfortunately, the actual sobering up is quickly glossed over in the movie, as if Jimmy had been cured over night.

Although the Mission got good publicity from the film, we took it very hard when Jimmy went on a drunk with his pay. We didn't know that it was his last fling. He visited an old friend, Denis Hadley, who was working for Nazareth House in Old Montreal when it dealt with hard core alcoholics. Denis got Jimmy into the Royal Victoria Hospital for his delirium tremens and when he came out, Denis worked on drying him out at the home, well away from the distractions of the Mission. Later, Jimmy made a pilgrimage back to Northern Ontario and took treatment at a clinic there. He has been sober ever since.

We met ten years afterwards and he said, "You don't suppose that I could work here at the Mission? I have my papers as a therapist."

We discussed it, but reluctantly agreed that it was best he kept trying in Ontario. Jimmy usually drops us a line once a year. Walk tall, Jimmy.

Bert's Bar

Not very far from the Mission there is a historic site called Bert's Tavern. Although they are now allowed in these bars, most women wouldn't be caught dead in this one. The management has tried about everything to keep the place open and thanks to the OBM, they have a ready-made clientele.

Their first promotional effort was to buy a large screen tele-

vision for sports and videos. It wasn't too long before porno-
graphic movies were the prime attraction. Then good old Bert
bought a coin-operated pool table for his clients' enjoyment —
and a little extra revenue, thank you very much.

In order to assess the kind of money available from their
OBM clients, little Ricky, one of our admission clerks, was
bought out; he jumped at the chance to make some easy tips.
He made up a list of those at the Mission who were on
Unemployment Insurance, Old Age and military pensions. Not
many men living at the Mission qualified for welfare in those
days, because they had no fixed address. All the others were
bad credit risks: they went into a black book along with the
undesirables. Ground rules were established and credit was
made available to all who were approved by Ricky; he was the
collector for Bert. As front desk clerk, Ricky handled the residents' mail and had all the power. He was also able to pad the
bills or demand tips from the boys as he chose.

Because I was in a new building and milieu, it took me a while
to catch on to this scam. In addition, Ricky kept feeding his
supervisor information about things that were going on at night
in the Mission, so he was a protected stool pigeon. I made it
known that "stools" were not my favourite people.

It was almost as if Bert could sense what was happening in
our internal investigation. He quickly started getting rooms
together for his better clients and moved to control their money.
Private rooms had no meal service, so he authorized a local
restaurant to allow the men to eat on the presentation of a chit
from Bert's. Some of our staff got upset over this latest move,
but give him credit — he was a real entrepreneur. At first I
thought this new scheme might be of benefit to the Mission
because now we could allow some new people in to take the
places vacated by Bert's previous patrons. However, once we
began to look into what they were doing, we decided it was definitely not advantageous to the "clients". All we could really do
was to block off the source at our end and clean our own house.
Once we fired Ricky, at least the cards were on the table and
we watched very carefully from then on.

There were so many incidents involving Bert's place over the years that I have the telephone number in my personal telephone directory. Perhaps the worst story concerned Bobby, who was a funny little fellow. With nothing better to do one afternoon, the lads invented a game, the idea of which was to see who could eat (or swallow whole) a pickled egg the fastest. The game went on for a half hour and Bobby was one of the best: not having a tooth in his mouth, he was pretty good at downing the eggs whole. While the fools were all laughing, Bobby fell to the floor gasping for air, an egg stuck in his throat. He died the next morning in Saint Luc Hospital.

~

Loan sharking businesses are not usually operated by the management of a tavern, it's just too risky. You could lose your liquor license and pay a very heavy fine. You can also lose a lot of customers, something tavern owners never want to do. That doesn't mean that money lenders don't operate in taverns — they do — and if business is really good, they may give the owner a piece of the action. Usually the money is spent right in the bar anyway, so the owner gets his action in any case. Normally you don't just ask for a loan outright; you sit down, watch the play, order a drink and then make the loan. At least one drink and tip goes into the establishment. At this point you're probably asking why in the world would anyone want to lend money to drifters on skid row? Bear with me and you'll see just how easy and profitable it actually is.

When people like the men who were on our Special Local Initiatives Projects get their pay, the major problem is trying to get them to practice moderation. They turn into big spenders and in so doing, become "marks" for the loan sharks; the interest rate is a minimum of five to ten percent a week — compounded of course — and you're off to the races. Not paying back can be a very serious mistake; these people don't play games. We were forced to hold back the week's pay until Monday because people who were paid on Friday evening, would disappear that night, leaving us in a hole for Saturday and losing us the money for work not done. We also had to establish a firm policy of no pay advances.

Chapter Six

One Sunday night while making the rounds of the Mission, I noticed a few of the men from the Project sporting bruised faces, bandaged arms and hands.

"That must have been a wild party Friday night!", I commented. All I got in return was a very sheepish "yes" from the men. When I got into the elevator, the night supervisor told me not to believe it, the collectors had caught up to them and they had all got warnings.

"Just how many do they have the arm on?", I asked. I was told it was all but a couple. I asked if this all happened at Bert's.

"Oh no, Rev. These guys all drink at the Capitol. There are women there and they try to outdo each other for the benefit of the girls. By Sunday afternoon or even earlier, the men are broke and if your foreman René gives a thumbs up, the guy can get a loan."

Well, they never taught me how to deal with that in the Seminary! I remember being told that we should read, learn and inwardly digest Holy Scriptures. Holy this wasn't and digesting it was tough. The whole project was coming apart just when we thought we were making giant steps forward. I was taught in my religious upbringing that these men's lifestyle was to be shunned, that it would in fact lead to Hell. These men were already living a hell on earth five or six days a week.

We had to pull the reins in very tightly. We blasted the men for their behaviour and let them know that we would not tolerate this style of life at the Mission. The infamous loan shark got a message that he was barred from the Mission and that if he was seen around the front door, we would call the police. By "coincidence", the foreman disappeared around the same time, along with a colour t.v. and a compressor.

~

Providing work for a man through programs like the Special Initiatives Project is one thing, but turning his life around requires social, physical and spiritual reinforcement if there is to be any progress. There was no question but that we had a responsibility to the Mission and to the community as a whole.

The next time an opportunity arose to try a new program, we

were ready. The Canadian penitentiary system asked us to put together a program for inmates on parole. However, when we presented it to them, we were told in no uncertain terms that no inmate would accept the kind of discipline we envisaged as a central theme and we would have to change various major elements of the program. We declined. Now, ten to twelve years later, we are seeing programs such as the one we proposed being initiated across the country.

We simply could not condone a program that allowed people to jump into perhaps a deeper pit than the one they'd been in before. I couldn't permit the men to be beaten up, even if it was essentially the choice they made by their actions, neither would I turn a blind eye to drunken and philandering lifestyles financed by Old Brewery Mission work projects.

~

Back to Bert's Bar. Around seven-thirty each night, the front desk would get a call to send somebody to pick up Scottie, who in addition to being very feeble, was almost blind, so a runner was always sent to bring the poor fellow home. This happened over and over again — we called it the OBM escort service. There were many old fellows in the same boat and they never really abused the outing, it was just that they simply couldn't navigate, with or without a drink. If they acted up, the tavern would simply cut them off and send them home, putting a bar on them for a few days or so.

So you think that total abstention is the answer? In response, I invite you to visit the front door of the Montreal General Hospital at minus 30 degrees Celsius and see how many people in night gowns leave the building in wheel chairs just to have a cigarette. Then imagine a man who has been drinking for fifty or sixty years, who's forced to live in a mission and knows that there is a tavern just a few doors away. Putting him out on the street just makes him homeless and might cost his life. I had enough on my back without carrying that around with me.

~

Chapter Six

Before the Mission moved to Clark Street, I am fairly sure that Bert never got involved with his clients the way he does now. However, when various businesses (pawn shops and restaurants etc.) were demolished for the Ville Marie Expressway, all of a sudden the neighbourhood was gone, so it became essential that Bert do something special to ensure the tavern's survival.

He got involved in finding rooms for his clients in one of the three or four major flop houses on the Lower Main, just above Vitré street (or Viger as it is now known). Bert found that some of them occasionally passed away in their sleep; he made a fuss about burying them — that was something he'd never had to do before. Still, every year Bert throws one Christmas party for "his boys" from the Mission and another one for the people from the newspaper La Presse and the workers from the Palais de Justice. There is also a sugaring-off party in the spring and a picnic in the summer; both require transport which old Bert pays for, along with the treats. It's the best deal in town, for a tavern that is.

Allen McInnes, The Gazette

The Three Amigos

Lenny

Lenny was a Merchant Seaman during World War II, an ex-boxing champion of New Brunswick in the 1940's and a very heavy drinker for almost thirty years on the streets of Montreal. The combination of boxing and alcohol made for a scrambled mind at a very young age.

Chapter Seven

Being a true dipsomaniac, it was a ritual for Lenny to be one of the first people out of the Mission every morning. By no later than five a.m., he or somebody in his gang would have been dispatched to a local bootlegger for a bottle of wake-me-up wine. By noon the gang would have a full glow on and Lenny would be into his second or third bottle of whatever the guys were drinking that day. You have to remember that the class of drink depended on the day's financial situation. If someone hit on some money, the rum or whisky would flow for days, until they had to fall back on wine and failing that, rubbing alcohol diluted with four or five parts water. That was Lenny's life, day in and day out, for over twenty-five years. Not surprisingly, the brain damage was extensive and Lenny could not carry on any type of conversation after one o'clock in the afternoon.

People say telling an ex-boxer he's punch drunk really hurts him. First because he's pained you could even think such a thing and second because he hates it that his condition shows. In Lenny's case, the compulsion to drink wasn't just a simple addiction, it was also a way to wash away the pain and mental blackouts he had every day. He would just lie down and sleep on the sidewalk until someone carried him into the Mission and put him to bed.

When I first met Lenny, he was the leader of the pack on Inspector Street. At that time, the standard drink was Bright's 440 wine in the gallon or 40-ounce bottle. When times got bad and funds very low, a delegation was sent up to a drug store on St. Lawrence Boulevard to purchase bottles of rubbing alcohol. Lenny used to say that this guy sold it by the truck load. The Montreal Police Department eventually put enough pressure on the druggists to pull the alcohol off the shelves, so the men switched to wine just as the Mission moved to the St. Lawrence area of Old Montreal in 1967. By coincidence, the price of rubbing alcohol rose dramatically.

Some fifteen years later, the Montreal Police carried out an investigation at our request into the sale of Chinese cooking wine, which sold for about three dollars a bottle, when the cheapest wine on the shelf was seven to ten dollars per litre. Technically this wine was innocent enough to be sold in grocery stores, but one litre of that stuff seemed to "cook" the minds of anyone who drank it. During the months before the police were able to convince grocers to restrict its sale to the local "Alcoholics Unanimous", the intoxication it produced generated some very gross behavioural problems on the street. Police had some very bad times just trying to subdue people who were drinking the stuff.

Lenny was always close to this action, but it was rare that he drank the Chinese wine, probably because some super organization of his own made this unnecessary. A very effective sub-culture had developed and a mix of panhandlers, petty thieves and runners managed to get other substances to drink and for the most part stayed out of trouble. Their main trouble was encroachment by outsiders and that was never tolerated. We used to laugh when a fellow from Dernier Recours bragged that he was King of skid row. Lenny and his boys had him beat by many years.

~

During the Mission's last years on Inspector Street and the next fifteen to twenty years in the new building on Clark Street, Lenny was one of the top winos on the street, with a code all his own. He would borrow and even steal a little, but he would proudly proclaim "I ain't no stool pigeon." No matter how serious the thing was, he would say "You know me, Rev. Even if I knew, I wouldn't tell you." But there were times when the situation was just too serious, when we couldn't let him get away with brushing us off like that and had to exert pressure. He would still refuse to talk. My only option was to bar him from the Mission completely for various periods of time, meaning he could not come into the building or use any of the facilities, including the bathroom. However invariably a week or so would pass, someone would report that Lenny was in a deplorable state, the ban would be lifted and we would start all over again.

~

Living on the street has its own health and sanitation problems. Once you reach the bottom rung, you are not allowed even to use the bathroom in a local tavern. By the end of a day or a few days at the very most, you begin to smell pretty badly. Lenny was one of the people who forced us to be strict about personal cleanliness. The other men at the Mission would complain that they could not eat when someone like Lenny sat next to them in the dining area.

Although we had always had a policy that newcomers had to take a shower on the first night they came to the Mission, we also had to invoke another policy of a minimum of a shower a week, more frequently if required. The trouble was, like most environmental problems, solutions cost money. We used to issue a towel per man per week and change towels and bed linen once a week, but the cost of replacing stolen articles was terrible, so each night we had to have a supervisor and someone to hand out and retrieve towels. And then we also needed someone to wash and dry everything the next morning. Despite the problems, we made the personal hygiene program mandatory. In general there was a marked difference between the behaviour and deportment of men at the Old Brewery Mission (OBM) and other missions, particularly Dernier Recours Montréal. The men complained that they didn't like the OBM because we forced people to take showers, get up at certain times and leave the building. Despite the opposition and threats, we maintained strict control of the shower program in all of our houses. In the beginning, men moved to other missions in protest, but when their time ran out there, they came back to the OBM and had to take a shower anyway, so things began to improve. But nothing is ever straightforward. We found that we had some less than brilliant staff, who could be counted on to do their best to turn things to their own advantage. Some were caught forcing people to take showers as a form of punishment. We put a stop to that sickness with threats of instant dismissal. Of course there is always a risk in letting damaged people try to heal themselves by working with other damaged people.

With the renovations to the Clark Street building in 1989, we had washers and driers installed on the top three floors and this allowed people to wash their own clothes. Instead of coin slots, we had electronic chips installed and this proved a good deterrent against theft until the staff person in charge of the daily laundry came up with a scheme to sell chips. It was months before he was caught.

~

Alcohol's powers depend on each individual's physical make-up. The central nervous system reacts when a certain volume of alcohol is consumed: the flow of oxygen is disrupted and legs become wobbly and unsteady. One very warm day, having had more to drink than usual, Lenny fell to the sidewalk and split his head open. The police drove him to Hôpital Saint Luc, which has a very high rate of unilingual francophone employees. For some reason, Lenny had a violent distaste for French people. Within moments, the Sister in charge of the emergency room threw him out of the hospital, calling him a dirty drunk and telling him to sober up and wash out his mouth, which was often very foul.

When my wife and I walked into the Mission, there sat Lenny on the bench at the front door, covered in blood and cursing "the lousy Frenchmen" at the hospital, saying they were all no good. I told him to be quiet and he calmed down. My wife washed his wound and applied a dressing. When she was finished, he looked up and said, "Merci, Madame Rev." After all that tirade, he could still acknowledge kindness shown to him in that other language. Unbelievable!

~

Clancy

Clancy and Lenny were good friends; they stuck together like glue, real gold-dust twins. They were the senior connivers during the first twenty-five years of my work at the Mission and if something was going down, you could be sure both of these two henchmen were involved. You might ask why I let them stay at the Mission so long. It's simple: the revolving door. The rounds began at the Old Brewery Mission, continued on to the Welcome Hall Mission, the Salvation Army, Bordeaux Jail and wound up at the drinking hang-outs on the mountain or in the back alleys before starting all over from the beginning.

Clancy's story was somewhat like Lenny's. He had held a

good job as a supervisor in a shoe factory but lost everything through alcohol. His wife, probably fed up with being left alone while her husband was with "the boys" at the local bar, dumped him. (The "boys". It's interesting, isn't it? These guys might be thirty, forty or fifty years old, but their adolescent behaviour never changes. When will they ever learn?) As time went on, Clancy sustained the same sort of severe brain damage as his friend Lenny. Clancy used to run messages for everyone and made a lot of tips that way, but towards the end, you couldn't even send him to the corner for a pack of cigarettes because he'd forget what he went for.

Friendship is not easily developed on the street. Things had to work well to turn people into buddies, drinking ones anyway. Clancy was accepted as a runner for whatever the boys were drinking. If he had ever failed to return with the goods, even leaving town wouldn't have saved him! For a good fifteen years, Clancy was also the principal schemer of the group of five or six. Lenny on the other hand was a little like a respectable Senator, nodding approval and saying "O.K. Boy, that's good! Let's go for it." We tried to break the pattern of their lives but never succeeded, because if one of them went to jail, his place in the group was waiting for him when he got out. You could bar Clancy from the Mission, but the next day he would be outside, waiting for Lenny to emerge.

There are hundreds of stories of stunts and outright scams pulled by this team of old delinquents who never got past being fifteen years old. One day Clancy was living above and beyond his means, someone having sponsored his Sunday afternoon in a bar on the Main above Dorchester. A pair of handcuffs that had probably been removed from some harassed policeman materialized. "Try them on me", said a grinning Clancy. When they couldn't get the cuffs off, the gendarmes were called. While checking his name, they discovered there was an outstanding warrant against him for non-support, ten years old but still in the computers. Clancy spent the rest of the weekend in jail.

Another case of bad luck: Lenny was sick and allowed to stay in the building for a couple of days. The cleaner on the fourth floor asked my assistant Mel Favreau for a ball of string, to line up the beds Army-style. Now good old Sergeant Favreau knew that there was no way that this mixed-up civilian could possibly have thought of using a length of string to line up beds, so he went to the window and spotted Clancy pacing to and fro below. Sure enough, the string was lowered to the street. Mel was on the third floor and as the rising bottle of wine got to the second floor, he cut the cord and the bottle smashed onto the sidewalk below. Unbelievable stunt. The two of them threatened Mel, but I promised them that whatever retaliation they planned, they would get back twofold from me. Like beaten dogs, they muttered but finally appreciated the masterful stroke of brilliance by the retired soldier who could anticipate most of their tricks.

~

The men who lived on the street day in and day out were never very clean because of the places they flopped and the way they shared their drink. Body lice were common and the men had to be washed and their clothes fumigated. The washing included a shower with Kwellada shampoo and Lindane body lotion, both liberally applied.

On occasion some of the men became not just carriers, but breeders of lice. Clancy became a breeder and had to be watched very closely. The lice were hard enough to control at the best of times, but whether to draw attention to himself or to smuggle bottles or other contraband, Clancy wore a winter parka all summer. You could argue all you wanted, but he would insist, "Rev, if it keeps the cold out in the winter, it'll keep the heat out in the summer." It got so bad one year that we put him out for most of the summer but then let him go to camp with the rest of the men. The deal was that before going to camp, he would shower and change all his clothes. We would issue him with similar clothing, including a winter parka. (The old clothes were dispatched with great haste to the garbage, enclosed in a couple of heavy duty plastic bags). Although Clancy had a natural aversion to bathing, we made it a ritual to have him showered at least daily. Whenever he became alive with body lice, the whole treatment would have to be taken. However the last time we went through this, we found he was infected in the groin area and had a huge swelling. After suffering more than necessary, he finally went to the hospital, where a blood test turned up a rare disease doctors thought had long since been eradicated.

The call went out. Two Mexican doctors appeared a few days later, examined Clancy and set about deciding what they could do for him. Once they got started, it was only natural that these distinguished doctors should want to meet with local experts to discuss the case. As the patient was mobile, not experiencing too much pain, had been most cooperative and had a good sense of humour, why not bring him to the case conference? The meeting was to take place at the Château Champlain, so the Mission got an urgent call for some clean clothes and a super suit was sent to Clancy by messenger.

Our man Clancy was about to reveal to these very expert gentlemen that he too was an expert. Within an hour, he had consumed all of their very expensive wine while they sat discussing his case. Brilliant thinking on Clancy's part, but a very stupid move. On the second bout of inflammation, Clancy died in the hospital. Many of us were very saddened by his death, but we also give thanks that no one else ever decided to do an encore on the parka act.

~

Bobby

Like Lenny and Clancy, Bobby was separated from his wife and determined to live as easy a life as possible: with few or no responsibilities, and as much fun as he could pack in. He looked about five foot nothing but he was actually about five foot six, wore a military-type brush cut for thirty years and in contrast to the others, was usually clean-shaven and well dressed. Bobby also had a good sort of a work record; you could send him out on odd house-cleaning jobs and you could hire him from time to time to fill in at the Mission.

One year, being on good behaviour in a rehabilitation program, Bobby was selected to work in the summer camp, as a kitchen helper and a general duty worker. He was our "sanitary Sam" and did a lot of cleaning and minor repair jobs. He'd also come over and cut the grass at my home and so have a few dollars to start the next day. My son and the campers in the Boys' Camp got to know and like him; they made him sing at the supper sing-along and he always had a kind word for the children. Once the summer camp ended, he was ripe for a few drinks and, with what he had left from his summer wages, was a great source of funding for Lenny, Clancy and "the boys". When the money ran out, he was the one in the best physical shape after having had a summer's drying out, so he became the runner for the group of winos.

That duty was a most solemn one and the person had to be very trustworthy to handle the group's assets. After the two-block run, there was a ritual to be observed: Lenny would fake popping the cork by hitting the bottom of the bottle with the flat of his hand, carefully unscrew the top — you'll appreciate that we're not dealing with classy wine here — and then solemnly say "The runner first" and Bobby would be allowed a regulation first drink.

After sharing a couple or so bottles, little Bobby would become very aggressive and when provoked in any way, acted if he was the champion fighter of the street, all five foot six inches of him. Many nice people become very bad and nasty when they've been drinking heavily. Bobby was one of these.

He used his deafness as a weapon when it suited him, saying with a straight face, "What did you say? I didn't hear you". One day Bobby went after everybody and insulted our admissions clerk. With my approval, he was refused admission until he sobered up.

"Big deal", said Bobby, lying down at the front door of the Mission and promptly falling asleep.

"He'll be pretty stiff when he comes to", I said, "so if he doesn't act up, you can let him in to sleep tonight."

The clerk agreed and said that he did not hold the incident against Bobby. He was just so drunk that something had to be done or there would have been a big brawl. My son Earle, who was about twelve years old at the time, had come to the Mission after school to ride home with me. We were leaving by the front door and there was Bobby in a fetal position on the sidewalk.

"What is the matter with Bobby?" Earle asked. I explained

that he had been a bad boy and couldn't go inside unless he changed his behaviour.

"You mean he'll sleep outside tonight?" I firmly expressed my hope that it would do him good after all the trouble that he caused that day.

"But that's our Bobby, Dad."

"Yes", I said, "let's go home."

"But Dad, you can't leave him here like this, that's our Bobby."

What could I do in the face of that imploring look? I opened the door and told Jimmy put him to bed and to bring him to see me in the morning: I wanted to make sure I could give him a good dressing down before the liquor commission opened at 10 a.m. and thereby take some pressure off the staff who had had their hands full the day before.

It was only a couple of months later that Bobby had a stroke and was admitted to hospital. We called his daughter who had on other occasions taken her dad home to try and get him back on the right track, but this time Bobby was under the control of the doctors. An application to have him taken care of at Saint Anne's Veterans Hospital was made and accepted. Had Bobby been released to the Mission and gone back to the street, his life expectancy would have been no more than a few months. With full care at the hospital, he had a good eight years more before he died. Each time I visited the hospital, Bobby was there as large as life, very grateful for whatever cigarettes or hand-outs he could get. Amazingly, the treatments and physiotherapy had him walking without any problem — he sure would have been up to his old tricks if he had been let loose on the streets. Mind you, it would have been lonesome for him because all of his original gang had passed away.

~

I was often asked how I could stand working with those hard cases day in and day out. The answer has never changed: they were all children of God, good and bad. My job was to try and bring out the good in them and surprisingly often, the goodness in them would break through, making our days a little lighter and better. If there was any reward, that was it.

B.B.Q.

It was Clancy who gave Caesar the nick-name "B.B.Q." and it was all because Caesar was unable to grow a proper beard. The best he could achieve looked like little wisps of fat on the side of barbecued ribs. The name stuck.

Chapter Eight

As it is for many of the immigrants who end up at the Old Brewery Mission, how Caesar got into the country in the first place was a bit of a mystery. We think his family arrived here from Romania either just before or just after World War II. There is little doubt that he had been psychologically damaged since childhood. When Caesar came of legal age, he was allowed to leave home and was probably committed to a mental institution at that point.

In the late 1970's and 1980's, there was a great exodus from mental care homes and hospitals and we at the missions became godfathers to all kinds of sick people. There is a huge difference between the chronic care costs for the mentally disabled in an institution and the care for the homeless provided at missions: $1,50 a day compared to $5. The cop-out from authorities was "We can't do anything unless they commit a crime." Caesar was one of those people who fell through the cracks and was released from a psychiatric hospital because he could function and was not dangerous. He was a perfect candidate for Dernier Recours Montréal as he didn't even know how to get on the welfare support list.

A few years ago, Caesar's eyes started giving him problems. After examination at the Reddy Memorial Hospital, it was found that he needed a cornea transplant. Plans were made for surgery, but Caesar wouldn't agree to the operation. Someone had stolen his cornea, he said, and he would wait until they gave it back. Under no circumstances would he let the doctor steal his eyes while he was asleep. Those mythological thieves were very much part of his world and had probably been with him since early childhood.

The hospital asked me to come and try to change his mind; this was the very hospital that had been maligned on an open-line show for its bad treatment of men from the Old Brewery Mission! Having practiced what I was going to say to him while driving the seventy-five miles into town from our camp, I thought I had a pretty good chance of convincing him. Unfortunately neither kindness nor fear would budge him. As you can imagine, I felt very inadequate.

Amazingly Caesar can still be seen going to the tavern, making his way by moving hand over hand along the cement wall and storefronts.

I Was in Prison and You Visited Me

It is really hard to work with someone who has been institutionalized and been made to fit an imposed pattern of behaviour. Deviations from those patterns are not acceptable to the institution, so prisoners have their own codes and standards to allow them to function in that environment. If their spirit is broken, then you have a real problem getting them to function in another milieu.

One of my first lessons about the role of the Mission in this respect came when the John Howard Society started calling to ask us to take care of people for them. After receiving many calls over a period of some months, I thought it was about time that they reciprocated and helped some of our men. I called the new Director of the John Howard, Stephen Cumas, and asked why he couldn't help a fellow who was just out of Dorchester Penitentiary. Mr. Smoothie replied he would rather not talk about it over the telephone, but why didn't I bring the fellow over and we would talk it over with him present. Good enough, I thought to myself, now we are going to see some action. Well, action I saw, but it was to be a lesson to me for years to come.

"Come on in Padre, nice to see you." It was like old home week, but a real pro was at work. "Have a cigarette," he said to me, then offered one to the lad just out of the pen. "No, thank you," the lad replied, even though his fingers were badly stained with nicotine. "How long were you in Dorchester?" "Twelve years" was the answer. (That was big time.) Steve asked a few more minor questions, the man shifting uncomfortably in his chair all the while, until Steve asked if he'd be more comfortable waiting outside. The fellow was out of the room like a shot.

"Rev," said Steve, "you guys are the miracle workers, not me. What do you want me to do with that fellow? In the pen they robbed him of his will to do anything on his own. Did you notice how he refused any kindness shown to him, how he was shaking for a cigarette and refused because he thought he was not good enough to smoke one of mine? He was unworthy in his mind to be in our company or to carry on a conversation; he wanted out in a hurry. He feels like a piece of dung because that's what they made him feel like over the twelve years. As an agency, we can supervise a certain number of parolees, but we can't treat and care for the really needy ex-inmates; we just don't have enough time to do the work that is needed. They are very damaged people."

It was a very valuable lesson. The truth was out, even if I didn't like it, so I just did the best I could with our wandering ex-inmate.

~

Over the next few years Steve Cumas and I became good friends. Imagine a hyperactive Greek and a renegade Irishman getting along! When he was lost for words, his theme song was "Damn it, you know...you're Irish", as if that had anything to do with anything. What it really meant was that I knew where he was coming from and he couldn't bluff me. Not that he really wanted to.

One day we went to a nice lunch together with our old friend, the Reverend Sam Pollard. But Steve was like a wild man. He went into a tirade, loosing language normally heard from his clients. "That crazy Gilhooly who works for me has been running book on the Society's telephone. The cops were in and they wanted to lock him up, but the cops won't have to punish him if I get my hands on him," he said. He'd really been taken in by a pro; Steve was always aware that almost any one of the smart crooks might just take him, which is why he played tough guy most of the time. Steve was actually laughing when he finished the story.

Criminologists have a multitude of terms they use to classify the inmates and once someone is rated on paper, he never escapes the prison of that classification. Primary Delinquent is the roughest one: since you were a terror when you were young, a terror you apparently remain. Violence and sex crimes, along with drug and/or alcohol addiction put you on the black list with the case workers, in prison or out.

Steve Cumas, Rev. Sam Pollard and I (a prison Chaplain for three years and a Commissioner on the Quebec Parole Board for five years) worked out that there were basically three kinds of inmates: about 80% are followers (or sheep, as old Sam called them); 19% are con artists; and 1% are professionals. It is that 1% who are the leaders of the human rights groups, work parties, anything that requires organization and allows them some freedom or a little time to speak to the warden or his deputies. The professionals have that all sewn up. One look at their clothing usually tells you that they are the executive class in the joint.

Sports and recreation are high on inmates' priority list and the power struggle to control them is remarkable. Money and influence mean everything, so the professionals and the top five percent of the con artists gain control of it all. They make mental notes on every prison employee and parole board member against a time when that information will be of some advantage. You may talk about the long arm of the law, but think twice before underestimating inmate power.

So just what chance do you think the followers have when it comes time to consider their parole? In the federal system, this war is fought on paper. By mail, the person is told that they do not qualify at this time due to various acts of anti-social behaviour, such as not informing on their neighbour and not cooperating with authority. Behaviour which of course will get you a bad beating or worse in prison. Anyway, these disqualifications leave the Parole Board time to study the cases of the professional or more educated type of individual.

Eventually mandatory parole kicks in; the poor souls must be released one day, so why not supervise them for the last third of their sentence? Chances of rehabilitation are extremely low and these men are candidates for the revolving door syndrome and missions like ours.

The answers are clear enough, but what civil servant or politician would agree to privatize some prisons, allowing inmates to work for standard salaries, pay room and board, support their families and most importantly, build up their self-esteem. We will have to wait to get into heaven to see that. It would be fitting if the selfish, laissez-faire powers-that-be were the first workers in that program. Be ye doers of the word, not talkers.

~

Much of street work is done with the cast-offs of life, most of whom are there by circumstance, not by choice. Unfortunately our justice system produces many of these people, bitter and angry because the system provides very little for the have-nots. Many a young offender never worked in his life and never had the desire or incentive to do so. Today many of our youth are becoming gang-oriented, with all the problems that involves. What are we doing about it? As usual, merely hoping it will go away. By the grace of God, there is a retired Roman Catholic Priest called "Pops", the Rev. Fr. Emmett John who is working in that not very nice wilderness. He would readily agree that the courts, prisons and jails fail to provide proper rehabilitation projects for these people, male and female alike.

While I was Chaplain in Leclerc Institute, a medium security prison, there were approximately 75 Protestant inmates, twenty to thirty of whom came to the chapel program, which included a choir that sang contemporary music as well as church music. There were also dialogue sessions on life in general. Looking back, only a very small number of these people were recidivists. We even had football games together at a park around the corner from my home after some of the men were released. When a police patrol car stopped once to watch the game, big Ray was heard to say "If they only knew who was playing here today." We all had a drink after the game and got together the next year. The point is that someone cared and only two or three returned to prison. Another couple paid the full price, being killed by enemies. Life went on. One day I was touched to find a verse among my keepsakes. Former convict no. B574 had given me a poem. I don't know where he got it from — it wasn't very good — but he meant it. It read:

So many men have tried, without success,
To save my soul, with "Brother, let us pray."
I fear that I'll not be there to answer "yes"
When someone calls the roll on "Judgement Day."
The pious word, the prayer, the psalmist's song
May bring my soul a momentary ease,
But peace that would be permanent and strong
Must come, it seems, by other paths than these.
And that's where you come in — not that you have wrought
My soul's salvation quite (for that is more than you have
tried to do), but you have brought
A hope to me that was not there before.
And all you've used to try to make me good
Is common-sense and kindliness and food.

If he were alive today, my scholarly pal, Sam Pollard, would be tickled by the deep thinking and say "We are merely instruments of God's grace." To which I reply "Amen".

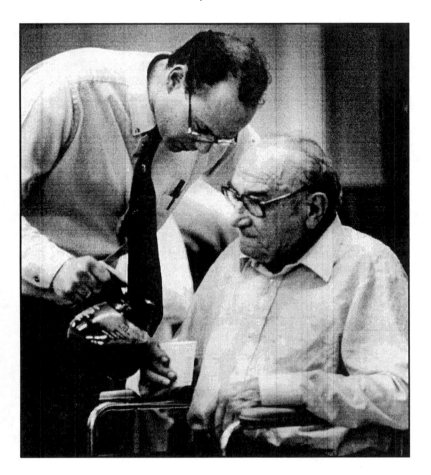

Bobby

There was a time when Montreal was the hold-up capital of North America. Banks didn't have access to today's sophisticated alarm systems, so the telephone and a revolver were the sum total of security. The Friday pay day was usually when the thieves made their withdrawals and hold-ups were so common, one sometimes had to wonder whether some of the institutions weren't just getting a little shortfall accounted for...

The robberies became so daring and the "takes" so large that the police finally organized flying squads to try and corner the thieves. A particular target was Bobby, a pretty tough little fellow and especially dangerous with a .45 revolver in his hand. He managed to elude capture and keep everyone guessing for several months. People got really tired of reading about how Bobby had once again escaped the police dragnet and the local newspapers hounded the police to shut down Bobby's gang. The whole town was petrified of the prospect of a Friday afternoon shoot-out on the streets of Montreal.

Of course Bobby's luck eventually ran out and he was sentenced to a long term in the penitentiary. When he left prison twenty years or so later, he was a physically and spiritually broken man. Incapable of finding a job, he eventually landed on skid row and would shoplift to get back into prison for the three meals a day.

While I was on the Parole Board as a Community Commissioner, Bobby's case came up. Bobby's record for the previous six years included minor loitering or shoplifting charges, hardly the big-time armed robberies of the 1950's. It was clear Bobby didn't have the faintest idea what parole was all about and didn't want it. On top of that, the full-time Board member wanted Bobby kept in jail prior to the hearing, as he was considered a very dangerous man. Naturally I asked why we were even hearing his case, but was told that it was the law and everyone had the same chance for parole. It seemed more than a little contradictory. On the one hand, the Parole Board did not like inmates refusing parole and on the other, all prisoners with a history of violence or armed robbery were to be considered a threat to society. On the way into the hearing, I told Bobby to say that he was not ready for parole and that is exactly what he did. Case closed. Ironically, Bobby was released from prison that very week because of overcrowding at the institution and came down to the Mission to live. He now attends A.A. regularly and is finding support and strength to carry on. He will not go back to prison; he lives in fear and trembling of it.

There can be no justification for Bobby's early crimes and no argument about the stiff sentence handed down. But the fundamental question is: what can be done for these people when they are turned loose on the streets, ill-prepared to deal with life after being out of circulation for so long? Until a better answer is found, helping hands like the Old Brewery Mission will be needed.

~

Fly Me to the Moon

There was always some especially bizarre behaviour on the street one particular day out of every month. No, it wasn't welfare cheque day, although that was bad enough. It was the eve of the full moon. The police, the missions and the radio stations could tell lots of stories about the crazy calls they had to answer on those nights. All the lonesome people seemed to congregate downtown and become temporary lunatics to swell the numbers of the usual actors and howlers. A person in that state of agitation will rant and rave for hours on end. It was extremely unpleasant to witness and I remember we often had to double the watch on those nights and call for help from the police.

There came a time when the psychiatric hospitals started to discharge people in great numbers because they were judged able to fend for themselves with medication. The drug addicts on the street welcomed these people with open arms and promptly stole their medication. We at the Mission began to see a high proportion of mentally-ill people who were not only homeless but in some cases, alcoholic and often very volatile.

Dr. Robert Shepherd was a well-known psychiatrist who visited the Mission once a week. Thirty to fifty percent of the men coming in suffered from a variety of mental problems, so Dr. Shepherd's help was greatly appreciated. He made it very clear to me from the outset that the majority of these men required long-term treatment and that not everyone could be cured. "Do what you can, make life easier for the men," he urged me, "and let them work out their problems with whatever help you can provide."

A good philosophy, but easier said than done because the men kept coming back for help. However, the good doctor was able to identify those people who needed immediate medical attention and he arranged for treatment as necessary. This was a real blessing: before that we could hardly get these men in to see a general practitioner, let alone a specialist.

During the height of Dernier Recours Montréal's activities, the Minister of Health accepted the fact that we had at least 100 very mentally ill people on the street and that some type of psychiatric support services were needed to cope with the problem. The average mission or street worker can manage just one or two sessions with these people a day. Any more drains them totally. Saint Luc Hospital being in the "war zone", it was commissioned to deal with the ten most difficult cases. The result? Of the seven people actually assessed, six would not cooperate so they were released and the seventh was an escapee from a

The Old Brewery Mission in the shadow of the *Palais de Justice.*

mental institution. End of program. What can you do?

To Serve and Protect

Recent reports about the Montreal Police brought back a flood of memories about their past kindnesses to men at the Mission.

My first memory dates from Christmas 1958. Two policeman had been assigned to the Mission to keep an eye on the men lined up by the hundreds for Christmas dinner. This was a sensible precaution because fights could easily have broken out and spoiled the day for everyone. Each officer took turns working the line inside and then the longer one outside. One of them stayed after dinner and put on a show, playing his accordion and leading the men in Christmas carols and other songs. To the men, that policeman was family.

And then there was the time a man at the Mission stopped breathing. We called the police ambulance, our only emergency support in those days. I had already started CPR and when the two policemen arrived with a stretcher, they immediately took turns trying to revive the man. What a tremendous feeling it was to feel his heart start up! Within a few moments he was on his way to a hospital, where he recovered. The thing that most touched me was that no questions were asked; the two officers sweated out the resuscitation of that poor old man and were thrilled with their success. I guess it's pretty rare that these fellows get to see happy endings — the fact is, you never call the police when things are going right.

~

We never kept count of the wanderers (or referrals as they are now called) who were brought in by the police, often in the middle of the night. These were usually poor souls the police felt didn't deserve to be locked up. One such case was a very simple-minded fellow who had just been released from a spell at Bordeaux Jail for vagrancy and given a bus ticket to get back downtown. With the idea of selling his ticket, he started to walk downtown but made a wrong turn at the front gates and ended up in Pierrefonds, exhausted, around 2:00 in the morning. He was given a lift downtown by the police and a bed at the Mission. Today all such men are released downtown.

~

I could tell you hundreds of stories, but there are two very special men whose kindness and support stand out. One was a simple traffic cop while the other ended up the "top cop".

This particular traffic cop was a special breed. His whistle, hand signals and stony stare could intimidate practically anyone into behaving, so if he actually spoke to you, you had really fouled up. However, behind that imposing mask was a man with a big heart. Jacques (a.k.a. Moustache) was assigned the area from St. Laurent to Bleury and St. Antoine to Viger. When the Mission moved to Clark Street in 1967, Jacques became the Patron Cop (Constable On Patrol). Over the years, Jacques got to know and care about all the men at the Mission, but we never realized just how much he meant to them until he showed up at the summer camp one day and the men made a big fuss over him and his young wife. "Hey, Rev! Did you see Moustache?" They were all breathless. The men later told us that Jacques always treated them fair and square, never harassed them and on top of that, was a good for a touch (temporary loan) once in a while. From time to time, Jacques had to speak to some of them about cleaning up their act — and they did. Because he was so effective, we occasionally asked him to have a few words with someone. If a really bad character got mouthy or nasty, he would be told to disappear or find himself in jail.

Jacques cared equally for the merchants and general public on his beat and was really friendly to everyone. Once, Jacques spotted a lot of smoke coming from a building at the corner of Lagauchetière and St. Urban Streets. After rushing upstairs, he led a group of very distraught people safely out of the building. He won his second medal for meritorious service that day.

Progress (the Palais de Congrès and one-way streets) eventually brought traffic lights to Jacques' corner, where once streetcars had trundled into the old Montreal Tramways Craig Street Terminus. Jacques (Jean-Jacques Laprade) retired early and became a painter of country scenes. He has done very well with his hobby and we hope it gives him some icing on that cake he deserves so much. He is missed at the Mission, on the Main, at the Journal La Presse, by the passers-by from the Palais de Justice...

~

There is another Jacques for whom I have a lot of respect. Captain Jacques Duchesneau (now Director of the Service de la Police de la Communaute Urbaine de Montréal) was a street-wise cop with many years experience as a detective when, during the second year of Dernier Recours Montréal, he became the Liaison Officer and a member of the Board. We were going through a really bad period in relations between the homeless of the inner city and the police. This very volatile situation was being recorded, filmed and fanned by the news media. Fortunately, the insights that Jacques was able to give to his superior officers and the local Station Director helped defuse some nasty confrontations. With the excellent liaison Jacques provided, cooperation and behavioral changes began to develop in earnest on both sides.

It is clear that his competence and efforts did not go unnoticed. Now in charge of the Montreal Police, Jacques Duchesnau is a very professional and human policeman. A couple of incidents in 1994 show that he hasn't forgotten his roots. One night he did a regular shift in a patrol car. Rumour has it that his young partner didn't recognize him. Afterwards, Jacques instituted a policy requiring all his senior officers to do the same to refresh their memories of what exactly is going on the streets of Montreal.

That same summer, Jacques threw his wholehearted support behind a project to provide sleeping bags to the homeless during the winter. Remembering what he had seen at Dernier Recours on Sanguinet Street, he saw a chance to do something good and acted. Of course some people saw the project merely as a Band Aid solution, but I always think that doing something today is more helpful than thinking about doing something tomorrow. Jacques went ahead with the project and provided warmth and comfort to many homeless men and women. We are fortunate to have a man of such high calibre at the head of our Police Department. Lâche pas, Jacques.

Yes, I know all police are not like these people I've described, but at least we ought to be thankful for the ones who are and be grateful that they are there when we need them.

Two Children of God

John

Late one year, a Veterans Affairs (DVA) social worker referred a disabled World War II veteran to us. We soon became painfully aware that John's artificiality went far beyond the prosthesis he wore.

The Mission was always swamped just before Christmas: everyone was taken up with preparations for serving 400 to 500 meals on Christmas Day and with putting together the 200 or so Christmas hampers for our Summer Camp families. During December, we also operated our own fund-raising campaign, which was run by Mission staff. Big Bad John was keen to get into the act too. He became very helpful to the night staff and even answered the telephone for the supervisor, who always seemed to be otherwise occupied. The next thing you know, John was volunteering to help out during the day too — and why not? He came with excellent references from the gang on the night shift.

Strange parcels began to arrive at the Mission, all addressed to John. It took us quite a while to figure out what was going down: John was soliciting gifts for the men at the Mission and then disposing of them or using them himself! We acted immediately, taking away his telephone privileges and removing a stock of Mission letterhead from his room. The parcels stopped coming.

The worker from DVA never warned us about his drinking problem, but we found out about it on our own soon enough. Around 10:00 one morning, one of the ladies in the office came in to see me and said there was a taxi driver outside waiting to be paid fifteen dollars. He had in his hands Big Bad John's artificial right leg, which had been left with the driver around midnight the night before as collateral!

A collective sigh of relief went up the day DVA called to say they had found a place for John in a brand new, low-cost housing unit for veterans. Pax vobiscum, Big John.

~

Bill

Now there was someone you would have thought had everything going for him, born and educated as he was in beautiful downtown Westmount. Unfortunately he was also a hyperactive person, impulsive and downright aggressive. The circumstances that brought him to the Mission were pretty amazing and it took us a year of interviews and conversation to put together the story of how this man become penniless and homeless through his desire to be wanted and fulfilled.

Bill was employed as quality control manager at a major printing company in east end Montreal. He met a girl who was living with her two children in a flat on the South Shore and seemed to be having difficulty supporting the young family on her own. Bill fell head over heels and before long, had bought a new home for them all. He thought this was going to be the fulfillment of his life-long dream.

To be fair, Bill was more than a little eccentric. While his companion went dancing, Bill did most of the household chores and acted as baby sitter. Once he was even beaten up by a couple of thugs and told to stay home and mind the children. According to Bill, soon after that incident he went into the bush behind the local subdivision with a set of air pistols for some target practice. Following on the heels of the beating incident, the girlfriend assumed that he was getting ready to shoot her. The police intercepted him as he came home and arrested him for carrying illegal firearms. While he languished in jail awaiting trial, Bill lost his house, "family" and job. The fact that one of the policemen was actively dating the girl probably contributed a tad to this mess!

For a few years after this incident, Bill was super-aggressive, but there was always that good streak in him that made his dilemma understandable and he did put tremendous effort into trying to put his life back in some kind of order. During this era, you couldn't collect welfare if you lived at the Mission, so Bill set his sights on becoming independent. He began by doing small jobs for us and quickly became the most sought-after handyman/cleaner we had. Once he had done household chores for someone — window washing or painting — the client would always call and ask specifically for Bill. He had his own room at the Mission, because we said if a man tried to help himself, we would offer extra privileges. Now the staff were mostly men trying to turn their own lives around and weirdly enough, that engendered a great deal of competition: they were not keen on other people getting ahead. So the bad reports against Bill rolled in, just because he was doing well. We did have to tell him to turn his ghetto blaster down when he insisted on playing the classical music too loud, but there again, the men at the Mission had a solution: they simply stole his machine. It became clear to Bill that it was time to move out. One day he asked to see me and told me that he had rented a room on Ontario Street and would appreciate it if he could drop in from time to time for any messages or mail. We shook hands and I wished him well and prayed that he would make it on his own.

Keeping in touch was easy because Bill was very thankful for the help he had received. Occasionally his room would be robbed and that would get him angry for a while, but he would always bounce back and come and talk to us about it.

There were times when he would show up with cuts and bruises all over his face. That was because he would get sassy with policemen when he tried to picket the courthouse with a sign decrying the lack of justice for himself. Eventually Bill got some advice from a public defender and bought a proper permit to demonstrate during certain hours, which he did faithfully in front of the Palais de Justice for weeks on end. Local newspapers wouldn't touch his story with a ten foot pole but they did write about him a year or so later when he died inexplicably in police custody. One might have suspected police brutality: Bill's police record showed charges for resisting arrest and he probably assaulted a police officer or two along the way, all of which must have made him as welcome as a skunk at a garden party. But the fact is that the disaster with the unfaithful woman and the local police on the South Shore had scarred Bill for life. He also suffered badly from epilepsy and without medication, would be in trouble.

Not all people on the street are drunks or drug addicts. Some are sad and unfortunate products of "the system". Every one of these troubled people should be offered a way to function normally in our society. The travesty is that during his trial, the experts declared Bill sane and offered no treatment. Sometimes the professionals blithely assume that people like Bill are just plain lying and want to get off lightly. In this case, society helped destroy a man. I think it is truly criminal that our legal system should insist you are not really mentally ill unless you

are a mad-dog killer with a machine gun.

Too Many Cooks

The idea behind a rescue mission is to help poor, homeless people over a short-term problem. You feed and shelter them, clean them up and turn them around. The food part of the equation gave us a lot of headaches over the years. After I had been at the Mission for about two years, we were lucky enough to get a new building. That, and the departure of the old cook, gave us opportunity to make some real changes in the way the kitchen was run. However, things didn't improve right away.

The first cook we had at the new Mission was Albert, who had moved with us from Inspector Street. He had trouble seeing past his nose, but he was clean and capable. However, the pressure got to be too great and we lost him in a tavern. The next fellow was well recommended as a former lake boat cook, but if he ever actually cooked on a lake boat, it's a wonder no one drowned him. The first week on the job he did a lot of frying and forgot to empty the grease pans under the grill, with the result that one day I looked out the window to see the firemen climbing a ladder into our kitchen.

~

Bob

What a relief when we eventually found Bob, an Army misfit who also happened to be a master chef. Cooking for a couple of hundred people necessarily means purchasing in bulk. It also often means a noticeable drop-off in quality. Unlike his predecessors, not only did Bob agree to use the bulk stock we had on hand, but his ability to improvise and make excellent meals with what he had was fantastic.

Bob's problem was that he was compulsive about everything, including his drinking. When he went off booze, he drank at least a case of Pepsi every day. When he took aspirin, he would down an entire bottle in 24 hours. As the pain progressed in his legs, he took 292's, as many as he could get his hands on.

Some of his stunts were classics. On my way out of the Mission one night, I noticed Bob at the registration desk, apparently examining residents' personal cards. Around 2:30 the next afternoon, I was told that the cook had disappeared and there was no one around to prepare supper. We found out that Bob was at Bert's Tavern on the corner, so I got someone to go and ask him to come and see me.

To roars of laughter, Bob answered, "Tell the Rev to come and see me in my office!"

It turned out that Bob was treating everyone who had said on their admission card that they had ever worked in a kitchen to free rounds of beer. Not a soul was left to help us.

Somehow our luck held. Just a few days previously we had made a deal with a meat wholesaler for a few hundred beefsteaks he was stuck with, for next to nothing. My assistant Don Waite and I took 150 of them from the freezer and started cooking: steaks in stewed tomatoes, potatoes, peas and carrots. To ensure that the news didn't get back to Bob and his gang, we allowed no one in or out of the Mission until the meal was served. After supper, the stoolies ran back to the tavern and reported to Bob that the men at the Mission were saying we had served the best meal ever. Bob was back in the kitchen at 5:00 the next morning, more than a little sick and very contrite. From that day on, I made sure that we always had five cases each of canned spaghetti, stew and beans tucked away in case we had another sneak attack.

~

Another of our chefs, originally from a downtown hotel, was such a good cook that we asked him to do a Board of Directors lunch. Somehow he convinced the supervisor that he needed a bottle of good Hungarian wine for a sauce. The meal was a great success and when I mentioned that the cook was a hotel chef, the President wanted to meet and congratulate him. Well, the cook came in, resplendent in his white uniform and chef's hat, doing a czardas and singing. Before his feet hit the ground, he was hustled out, still singing and feeling very happy on the three quarters of a bottle of wine carefully left over from the sauce. The Lord knows I really tried but I lost a few on the way.

~

Johnny

There were times like Christmas, Easter and Thanksgiving when we had to bring in outside support. Johnny, whose wife and children had attended our summer camp for many years, was always ready to lend a hand for special occasions. Johnny would have loved to work with us permanently but he was getting workman's compensation and was awaiting a final settlement; to have accepted a job would have stopped the process immediately. One Christmas we asked him if he could prepare five to six hundred dinners for us. He agreed on the spot and worked every night for a week, producing one of the tastiest and most successful dinners in years. Eventually his old injury became more painful and he had to stay home. He was a very capable man and we missed him long after his departure.

A nice young fellow working at a lunch counter said he had heard we were looking for a cook. He seemed ideal: married — not a skid row type — with his own place. We took him on and

things seemed to be working out quite well, except for one little problem — he was apparently carrying a little bag of good-
ies home each night. I instructed the staff to watch and let me
know if this practice continued. Being an outsider, he had no
friends to warn him to clean up his act, so ten days later he was
intercepted on his way out the door with enough food in his bag
for several days. He was fired on the spot. Ironic that the guy
who turned him in was an even bigger crook! Unfortunately
incidents like these occasionally happen. Sometimes it's a set-
up and you have to be quick to figure out if someone is just
after the job or wants to throw mud at a different department
to take the heat off themselves. Far too often I saw people
painting someone else black, to hide their own greyness.

~

Once I was talked into trying out a Social Sciences student
from Sir George Williams University. We chatted about what
hours he would like to work and I was pleased when he replied
"In the evening, when the men are here." However, it wasn't
long before the Admissions Clerk and others reported that this
guy wasn't respecting the way things were done at the Mission:
he was insisting on eating with the men and so on. The lad's
every move was watched relentlessly by other staff members.
Frankly, I thought it wasn't such a bad thing to have the rou-
tine challenged, so I resisted the harping and sniping as long as
I could, but eventually the staff got to me. "The guy is a dirty
big slob", they said. "He doesn't even wash, let alone shave."
They knew they were making headway on this poor fellow and
they wouldn't let up.

By now I was concerned, because the student was ignoring all
my rules for the staff. When I asked him what he was trying to
achieve at the Mission, he said that he was trying to get close to
the men and was convinced that by eating with them and looking like them, he could turn a lot of them around. I told him that
I was facing a staff rebellion for allowing him to do the very
things that I had forbidden them to do and furthermore, that
this style of working with the men was definitely not what I
wanted adopted at the Mission. Condescending to people is very

dangerous. Maybe the only thing some of these people have left is their pride, so you must not degrade them by going down to their level. If they can respect you for what you are, then we have a chance with them. The student was upset, felt that he was not being appreciated and decided to leave then and there.

~

Kevin

One day I wondered if my assistant, Mel Favreau, had flipped out. "Melvin", I said, "blow that one past me again. You want Kevin to work in the kitchen?" Kevin was someone I considered rather anti-social.

"I know, Rev", Mel said, with his eyes gleaming, "but he is just the guy we want in the kitchen as a dishwasher. No one will interfere with him and no one will try and push him around. Rev, I tell you, it's perfect. We can't go wrong. Kevin is just the settling influence we need in the kitchen."

I still couldn't believe what I was hearing. Kevin had lived at the Mission for about ten years, doing absolutely nothing and if he had said ten words in all that time it was a miracle.

"You'll be sorry", I predicted. "There'll be a big explosion and someone will get hurt; those silent waters run deep. But if you want him, Mel, you can have him."

Well, to tell you the truth, Kevin turned out to be one of the cleanest and best kitchen workers we ever had. His clothes were always sparkling white, he was clean-shaven, hair always neat and nicely combed. More than that, the kitchen was almost immaculate. These are usually the trademarks of an alcoholic trying to get the demon out of himself, but we never had any trouble with Kevin drinking. This man who had been declared retarded by his peers decided at the end of his twenty-sixth week of work that he was entitled to Unemployment Insurance and that he was going to collect it for the next six months or so. Kevin never worked another day in his life and died in bed at the Mission a year later.

I Was Hungry and You Fed Me

The Supper Club

Frankie was a very quiet person, seeing everything but telling nothing. He seemed have all kinds of knowledge and wisdom ready to explode out of him. That's why Frankie was selected to be a member of the Supper Club, a group that met once a week as a therapy program. The first half hour we enjoyed a good meal, then we got down to business. We always started off with what everyone had done since the last meeting; everyone had to speak for a few minutes. The next question was, had they looked for a job? Finally, how were they coping with their problems? Sometimes the reports got a little embroidered.

One night Frankie couldn't stand the fabrication any more. "Bullroar! You were sitting in Atwater Park all week. I saw you!" There was another fellow who went into an act about alcoholism, damning A.A. in the process. His message was that you have to have personal fortitude, a job, money and psychiatric treatment to help you over this terrible demon. Frankie shouted his disagreement. "Baloney! I was a drug addict on the Main in the 1920's and I broke the habit. I was an alcoholic in the 1940's and I overcame that. When I took sick in 1961, I lost everything: job, apartment, clothing, furnishings — the whole kit and caboodle. In two years, I will get my Old Age Pension and I will be out of here. Just consider yourself lucky, young fellow, to be young and healthy. Just maybe you might find the tools to finish the job."

There was great fellowship in that original group and it was a bold experiment that changed some lives. There was a fellow named Ernie who was at one time a mechanical engineer, ex-RCAF officer and alcoholic. He was the first one to find employment, but he stayed with the group anyway and helped out a great deal.

A few years later as I was walking on St. Antoine near Beaver Hall Hill, a large tractor trailer pulled up beside me and the driver hailed me. I looked up in astonishment. "I don't believe it! Ernie! What are you doing driving this monster?"

"Well, thanks to you and the gang at the Supper Club, I got my act together. I am back with my wife and very happy to have a job that doesn't give me the kind of pressure and stress I had in the construction world."

~

There were lots of people who wanted to help out at the Mission during my time there. It was difficult to put a program into effect because you had to train volunteer personnel and teach them how not to get taken to the cleaners by the men at the Mission.

The President of the Lakeshore Civitan Club was a family connection of mine. He knew all about the Old Brewery Mission and thought that it would provide a good hands-on project for club members. So we instituted an annual special roast beef dinner in late January, when all the Christmas activities had ceased. The total cost of the meal was around $250 but the club gave us $750 the first year and they came and served the food. As of 1993, they had been doing this for fifteen years, donating at least $1,000 per year for the meal. There was a additional minimum $1,000 for the Summer Camp after the second year. That idea caught on with other service clubs and we now suggest it as a way for people to see what is happening to their money at the Mission.

Mr. Bob Mariani, a local insurance man, was manager of the Quebec Region for London Life of Canada and a member of Lakeshore Civitan Club. He felt that some of his young staff had no real understanding of what it was to be without food or clothing and he got his staff to serve a dinner one night at the Mission. Over the next few years the staff took up a collection among themselves and served a series of dinners. Bob's main idea was to help his young staff get a different perspective on life. Their salaries were excellent but gambling, parties and alcohol were starting to cause problems in their families and Bob wanted to shake these people up through the dinners at the Mission.

~

The end of the month was a tough period because all the men were broke and needed help. The president of the N.D.G. Branch of the Royal Canadian Legion, Percy Mackay, came up with the idea of sending volunteers at the end of each month to help serve the meals. They have maintained this practice for seven or eight years now. It is an all-round blessing, since it keeps Mission staff alert, ensures that no sloppy meals are served and that the kitchen and dining room are clean.

~

Concern for visitor-volunteers got me in big trouble one time. Some 25 women from Bell Canada put on a tremendous Christmas party, dinner and gift presentation: new socks, rubber boots, woolen gloves and many other things for each man. The problem was that the women had no concept of some of the men being infested with body or hair lice; they insisted on serving each man at the table, reaching over and taking a real chance of catching lice. How do you gently warn these kind people of the risk? All the ladies wanted to do was to show kindness and friendship to some pretty friendless people, but I knew the closeness of two hundred men and twenty-five to thirty women in one cafeteria was asking for trouble. Thank the Lord, there were no problems, but some of the volunteers were angry with the way the event took place.

Fortunately an old friend from the Fusiliers de Montréal was a director of the Bell welfare fund and he explained to them why we had to enforce precautions. From then on, we advised people ahead of time what to expect and how to handle themselves in every situation.

Playing horseshoes at Camp Chapleau   *Len Sidaway, The Gazette*

Men's Summer Camp

At the Senate hearings on poverty during the 1970's, one of the committee members asked why we didn't take the men of the Mission up to our camp. (The camp's objectives had always been multi-dimensional, but it was primarily intended to give mothers and children from the inner-city a really super experience.)

"Because we never thought of it," I replied. For years afterward I was plagued with the idea, but never moved on it.

Then one day, a City of Montreal health inspector presented me with the results of his inspection of the Mission kitchen. He wanted to know why we had milk from Lowes Dairy, which was in Lachute. Had we brought it down by refrigerated carrier? I explained to him that this was a one-time only occurrence and that we brought the leftover food from the camp to give the men at the Mission a treat. Luckily we got off with just a warning, but it made me think. Why not take the men to camp and finish off the food on site? Why not use the time to look at the men as individuals to see what the Mission's winter program ought to be? We had the staff and we had the food. There were other expenses of course, but it would give us a chance to close down one floor at the Mission for 10 days and clean and repaint it without putting anyone out.

~

The Mission staff had all agreed that with the men at camp, we should have very few problems. However a few men rebelled at going and would absolutely not move. In addition, the office staff had no intention of taking their vacation during those two weeks and things didn't look too good.

I had other worries as well and was beginning to realize that it was one thing to write up a program and another to implement it. My wife noticed my nervousness just before we left for the camp and asked me about it.

I said, "What happens if a man dies in camp? Will we be sued for negligence?"

Colette thought a moment and then said, "What do you do in the city when a man dies?"

"I call the police", I answered and so settled my own biggest fear. How could I know that in a week's time, calling the police was exactly what I'd be doing?

That Thursday evening we had a spaghetti dinner. Everyone had a marvellous time eating to their hearts' content, but one fellow couldn't seem to stop packing it in. He must have eaten five plates worth and had a heart attack in his room later that night. We tried without success to revive him and called the Provincial Police in Lachute. About a half an hour later, the police pulled into camp in a cloud of dust, wheels spinning.

"Who touched the body?", a policeman demanded.

He didn't seem satisfied with my answer that we had tried to revive the man and things started to look nasty. Fortunately, when I took him up to the dining room where his partner was talking to someone else, the second policeman recognized me and was able to explain what the Mission was all about.

We contacted the man's next of kin through the police, but they told us that the wife wanted nothing to do with him and we could bury him if we wanted to. The Mission paid for the funeral, I took the service and the parish priest at Pine Hill gave us the free use of the cemetery. Within a week we received a telephone call asking for a death certificate so that his wife could collect death benefits from the Régie des rentes du Québec...

By ill luck, we were expecting a visit from the Board of Directors the day after the fellow had died. The Directors wanted to see first hand how the men were adapting to camp. It was supposed to be an upbeat type of day with the men doing their thing and enjoying themselves and me explaining to the Board the kind of projects we wanted to undertake for the next year. Naturally we wanted to show how well things worked and how contented the men were, but we were a somewhat subdued bunch.

"By the way", asked the President, not missing a thing, "wasn't that a morgue wagon we met on the way into camp?"

What a way to begin an inspection by the brass! I allowed as how it had been a morgue wagon and told him the whole story, assuring him that we had done everything necessary. That taken care of, we went on with the visit and the Board got a pretty good idea what we were doing in the camp that year.

~

Once we had the men in camp, the benefits were immediately obvious. For the Executive Director, being on site meant he got up to date quickly on the state of the men and gained insights on the future requirements of Mission programs and policies. Most of all, he was able to establish a relationship with the men that made them feel like human beings. The tight cliques of informers and muscle were broken up and one-on-one contacts were made.

The important thing was getting to know first-hand just who were the doers and who were the talkers. Sitting in my office and directing traffic through supervisors with their own agendas was never my approach. Getting opinions from intermediaries who had no idea what real people were all about or from those who relied on informers is basically bad management.

The men who steered clear of conversation usually had some kind of secret. However at camp, quite a few developed enough trust to let us into their confidence from time to time and it was all because we ate the same food at the same time and even in the same room. All little things, but they added up.

In principle, the camp could provide an excellent opportunity to retrain people but that requires broad support from staff, which I was never able to successfully muster. They never fully believed those people were reachable. Nonetheless, during those summer days we identified a few people who wanted to make progress, had some inherent ability to work with the other men and were willing to help others.

~

Taking 150 men of unknown ability from an urban environment into a rural campsite was an enormous challenge. Fortunately the necessities of life were provided, including regular toilets! The rules of the place were very simple: no smoking in the dormitories; make your bed and clean your room by noon; and be washed and shaved by lunch time. You could sleep in if you wanted but you had to turn up for lunch. People selected their own table to eat at and if someone missed the second meal of the day, someone else at the table had to report his absence.

With three meals a day, coffee breaks morning and afternoon and a bedtime snack at 8:30 p.m., keeping the cooks happy was essential to a smoothly-running camp. Some of the cooks were paranoid that we'd find a replacement for them if they took time off, so we were very careful how we approached it.

"We have to discuss the menu, cookie. There are a few changes I would like to make."

"You're the boss" was the usual answer.

I staked out my territory. "All right then, Sunday morning breakfast is my specialty. The men are usually up around six, so the kitchen will be open from 06:00 hrs. to 08:00 hrs. The night watchman will turn on the coffee urns and the stoves an hour ahead of time. I and one or two volunteers will cook a special breakfast for the men."

In the beginning the cooks thought this was a big joke and we'd never pull it off. They were wrong.

As long as you came in between 6:00 and 8:00, you could line up, place your order and be served a hot meal within minutes. This went on for fifteen years and the men often talked about it back in the city. The menu was bacon and eggs any style, hash browned potatoes, a couple of slices of tomato, fruit juice, cereal, toast, coffee, milk or tea. On Wednesdays we made pancakes with syrup and the men loved it. For lunch that day we served cold cuts and tossed salads and a bowl of soup; spaghetti with meat sauce for supper. This gave the cooks a good twenty-four hours out of the kitchen.

We also gave the men lots to do. In the evenings, we held cribbage and 500 (similar to whist) tournaments and the favourite — bingo — complete with prizes. You name it, we invented it, right down to a variety hour when mouth organs and spoons appeared and there was folk dancing along with singsongs led by the old army sing-along champ — meself. We also offered boating, swimming and canoeing and set up two horseshoe pits. Two very quiet men were often seen practicing at the crack of dawn. They became the ones to beat, meeting — and trouncing — all challengers. The championships were another kettle of fish for Kevin and his crew. They lost every year, despite winning on almost every normal day. The key to success was to rattle them while they played and the opposition was very good at that. The game became a psychological drama and tight-lipped Kevin would steam with anger at the remarks while he was playing. He'd lose his concentration and get talked out of winning. Maybe a kindly old coach should have thought of ear plugs...

Chapter Fifteen

As I look back on it, the days at camp gave the men lots to think about and to do. We even had professional variety shows. Frankie Munro of Saint Anne's Veterans Hospital fame put together a cast of show people for the last fourteen years I was with the Mission; the performers would come to camp, have supper with us and then put on a wonderful show. Jimmy Stevens, a very talented young man, always supported Frankie with his guitar and lively Irish songs as well as with a sound system that everyone could use. We even had Geraldine Doucet. Bill Snow, a yodeling champ of the early 80's and a western folk singer, always got me to sing a duet with him to close the show. (More than likely it killed it, but they were always nice to me). We solicited quite a few dollars from my friend at the Erin Sports Association, Jimmy Barriere, to finance the show and the men appreciated everything.

~

Rehabilitation Program

Despite the activities, many of the men were restless and wanted to do some work, so we set them jobs like painting the cabins in the boys' and girls' camp and even the big buildings like the Main Dining Room and the two story R lodge. Sweating a little with the men, showing them how to mount scaffolds and how to paint, brought us all closer and the men could better relate to me back home in the city.

Over the years, giving projects like that to the "campers" became less and less feasible because the work went to a special rehabilitation project we started for ten men (known as the "rehabs") who worked for a salary from the Mission. We tried desperately to hire someone to oversee the project who could inspire these men to reach for higher goals and change their life-styles. What we really needed was someone to live on site and work alongside them, because when things go wrong, the leader should step in and take the time to show the men how to do things properly. What we actually got were supervisors who allotted the jobs and then retired to their cabins, only to come out yelling when the work wasn't done.

Eventually we were able to find a foreman who wasn't afraid to work with the men and show them what to do. The problem was that he lived in Montreal and though he arrived in camp by seven each morning, he would be gone by two in the afternoon. The men's enthusiasm waned after he left each day. It was only a matter of time before all the employees wanted his hours, even if they could only do ten percent of what he did in a day. The situation worsened when the foreman's nephew came to work and only put in five or six hours a day.

The idea of the rehabilitation project was good but its execution was poor, mostly due to lack of day-round supervision. When the cat's away, the mice will play! However, we wanted so much to believe that we could provide a worthwhile program that we allowed it to continue. Campers' participation in work projects was then naturally limited. However a few years ago, the rehabs were doing a woodcutting project, with no hope of being able to split some 350 cords of wood in time for the fall sale. We organized four work crews from the camp to split and stack the wood on pallets. The work was completed in two weeks at a cost of $2,000. We realized a profit of close to $15,000!

~

Jacky and Louis

One of my favourite camp stories involves our annual Spring clean-up. Rescue missions are much like prisons in the springtime; everybody gets the fever. In our case discipline begins to fall apart. Personal deportment degenerates and the drinking bouts intensify. It's a bad time to try and put work teams together, but we simply had to do it or hire contractors at high cost.

Jacky and Louis were two very clean fellows who were pushing brooms at the Mission for extra favours, such as being allowed to stay in the building all day while the other men were turned out to find jobs. When we asked for volunteers to go up north to the camp, they showed great interest so we planned to have them head up the new work team for the camp foreman.

The strange thing was that every attempt to get official identification for these two failed. The first inkling we had that something was not right was when, after having said that he would love to go to camp, Jacky announced that he was a Chinese citizen and had to have permission from the Embassy in Ottawa to go. (He was not Asian, more likely middle European.) Since our experience was that when one person jumps ship, others follow in rapid succession, it was imperative to head this off. My assistant said it was no use talking to Jacky, his mind was made up and he wouldn't go unless he had the paper. So we manufactured an official permission to move about the Province of Quebec under the supervision of Major McCarthy, C.M., C.D. We photocopied a picture of the Korean Military Attaché from a Korea Veterans Magazine and got a Chinese merchant up the street to sign the "permission", just in case by some strange chance Jacky could read Chinese. So Jacky went to camp after all.

Louis was also very unusual. He claimed to be a distant relative of the late Louis Saint Laurent, Prime Minister of Canada in the early 1950's. Once, both men were brought back to spend the weekend in town. During their absence, I organized a work party to split wood so that we could sell it the following winter. When Louis came back to camp on Monday morning, he reported the theft of four thousand one hundred and thirty-two logs from the wood pile. I had to assure him that the wood he saw in the crates had been split and packed over the weekend and if he cared to count, he would find at least sixteen thousand pieces of wood. Nobody was going to steal our wood with Louis on the job!

We decided in the end that both were escapees from mental institutions and were just brilliant in covering their tracks.

~

What you don't know...

I'll never forget one new fellow who came to camp, trying to dry out while he was laid low. He had been just released from the penitentiary and was drunk for a month before coming to the Mission and signing up to go to camp for ten days. The bullies started pushing him around a bit, but they were flirting with big trouble. In a matter of days, this big fellow grew stronger and soon had everyone afraid of him. He must have spent his time in prison pumping iron in the gym, because his arms were the size of an ordinary person's legs. He won all the sports events — even the card championships!

Eventually he decided the camp was his and marched around doing exactly as he pleased, acting like Rocky. The staff couldn't handle him and the men were terrified. It was clearly time for a man-to-man talk and fearless me put the cards on the table. My one-sided talk went like this:

"We have rules to protect everyone and if you can't follow them or don't want to, the highway is just a mile down that road. You can leave any time." Amazingly, he apologized and toned down for the last few days.

Three months later, someone brought me a news clipping: the same fellow had been sentenced to life for killing his room-mate over a bottle of wine.

"Self", I said "you'd better not be so daring in the future".

~

Napoleon

There was a jolly fellow by the name of Napoleon, who had been working in the Mission as the night watchman. At that time, he was huge — tall and very heavy — and we had no worries that anyone would be dumb enough take their life in their hands by challenging Napoleon during the night shift. However, because of illness, he eventually retired and lived permanently at the Mission. Within hours of arriving at camp for the first time, he wanted to go fishing, so we came up with a couple of Canadian Tire fishing rods so the boys could have a crack at it.

Napoleon started appearing at the kitchen door with six or seven sunfish he'd pulled out of the lake, asking the cook to prepare them for the boys. The fact that his request was regularly refused didn't stop him coming back every day for the whole ten days at camp. The following year Napoleon brought his own rod, thank you very much, and again plagued the cook with a pail of fish each day. He was determined, you had to give him that.

After returning from camp one year, he went into the hospital with cancer, but he never really knew what was wrong with him because when we asked him about it he'd say, "You know, Rev, I have to go to the hospital for three weeks and all they do is take my picture."

When he showed me the indelible pencil trace lines on his body, it brought back memories of the cobalt treatments that my first wife underwent. It was a long, hard struggle for a lovely old fellow and thanks to a friend of ours, Lucie Myre, he had some good friendship during his last months.

~

Nick and Stanley

Nick was another fellow who was obsessed with the lake. From dawn to dusk, he would row a boat from one end of the lake to the other, back and forth. It almost seemed that he was rowing to freedom as back and forth he went, day in and day out, in wet weather or fine. He seldom spoke to anyone and never seemed to mix with the others; we just let him row.

Then there was Stanley, the painter. He wanted to come to camp to paint — anything that needed painting he was willing to do. The only problem was that Stanley couldn't stop talking. He just seemed to go on and on. Being unilingual, he had to work with someone who could understand English, but that was a problem because his reputation as a talker preceded him. The average worker could only stand to spend a day at most working on Stanley's crew, so I was the happy volunteer. To tell the truth, his stories were pretty interesting and we managed to get more painting done than the other teams.

~

Better the Devil you know...

While we were considering in the early days how to manage the camp, we were very much aware of the impossibility of keeping it "dry". We knew that some of the donors to the Mission would be very upset at the thought of their money going to buy beer for the men, but we also knew that these fellows would walk a hundred miles to find some booze. I confess that we started to serve two pints of beer a day.

Mr. Clifford Powell donated the first thousand dollars and a good friend gave another thousand. We also got twenty cases — or two days' ration of beer — free from Labatt's Brewery, thanks to the tavern on the corner. Year after year, we were able to raise the money for the men's summer camp via golf tournaments, shows and so on.

Weaning the men off their usual daily consumption and getting them down to a subsistence allowance was a major feat, but we were able to do it without too much trouble. There were isolated cases where we had to give a fellow a drink first thing in the morning, but usually by the second or third day, he would bounce back.

We did have a few bad cats who walked the five miles to beautiful downtown Sixteen Island Lake or to the village of Laurel. In both instances, relatives of the camp caretaker would call and let us know that one of our boys had just bought a case of beer and was sitting by the roadside enjoying himself. We weighed each case on its merits and decided on discipline. Essentially the choice was between making — and keeping — a serious promise to try again or being subject to a swift return to the streets of Montreal.

The amazing thing was that after the first summer, the men as a whole cut back on their drinking two weeks before going to camp and the behavioural problems were really negligible. One man who had been a very aggressive and antagonistic drunk ever since he came back from the Korean War actually stopped drinking altogether to go to camp and ten years later, still hasn't had a drink.

~

There was only one year that I had some really bad vibes and a sinking feeling that things were getting out of hand. Unfortunately, the person who usually took and screened the applications for camp had been sick that year and didn't have control over the selection of campers. As a result, we had many undesirables. The two-week camp was rapidly coming to a close, something was definitely wrong and I knew I had to make a move. Anyone who has ever been to camp can appreciate that the last night can be quite an experience. There was electricity in the air and something didn't smell right to me. Having witnessed a penitentiary riot as a chaplain, I had terrible visions of bad things to come.

After talking with the staff, I decided to move the evening closing banquet up to the lunch hour. We would make all the awards and speeches then, bring the buses in around three p.m. and send everyone back to the Mission, where we could more easily control the situation and defuse whatever was going down.

The men were shocked when the buses pulled in to take them home, but I am convinced to this day that we did the right thing at the right time.

The Arthurian Legend

During the 1950's and 60's, a lot of Maritimers were coming through Montreal on their way to Toronto and points west, many of them going to jobs lined up with the help of family or friends. All the trains provided for a long stop-over at Montreal and everyone had to change to continue on. Unfortunately, quite a few of these people never got back on the train and wound up at the Mission.

At that time, drinking establishments were relatively new in Halifax and Sydney, so you can imagine the revelation of this city with a tavern on almost every corner. Then too, someone would invariably have told them that when they got to the Big City, they had to see the Main (St. Lawrence). Life on the Main was as fast as anywhere in the world and it often took less than 24 hours for a fellow to lose everything he owned, forcing him to find his way to the local missions until he could get enough money together to get out of town. That's how I eventually met Arthur.

~

Arthur on the Street

He was no king, but Arthur was a very gifted man who, in the face of tremendous problems, found his solution early on in drink and laughter. As the years went by, the lifestyle took its toll: his drinking became an obsession, his wife and family had had enough of him and his body was racked and ravaged by alcoholism and tuberculosis. Arthur also spent some time at the Royal Victoria Hospital, undergoing treatment for injuries sustained during the Springhill Mine disaster. You'd think that he'd want to avoid further suffering, but he just couldn't seem to change the way he was living. Financially strapped, Arthur learned about the Old Brewery Mission from people on the street and dropped in to see us.

I should explain that not having money was never reason enough to stop drinking. You just downgraded the quality of alcohol, first to wine, then rubbing alcohol or Chinese cooking wine. (In Montreal, we don't seem to have the same magnitude of problem that Ontario cities have with people consuming rubbing alcohol or Lysol, perhaps simply because here the dépanneurs — convenience stores — can and do sell beer and wine until 11 p.m. every day.) In those early days of the 1960's, Arthur's first solace was Bright's wine, but in the big 40-ounce bottle, not the puny litre size we have now. Then he was introduced to rubbing alcohol. Rubbing alcohol mixed with four parts water makes about 80 ounces of a very powerful intoxicant, enough for four or five men to get stone-drunk, aggressive and down-right nasty. They were real pests then and you couldn't allow them into the Mission for fear they'd start a riot.

Our friend Arthur tried every kind of drink and indulged in

every type of poor behaviour imaginable, yet there was still something basically likable and true in him. Having served in Korea with many Maritimers, I had a real soft spot for him and so did other people. Many drunks would be left to fend for themselves if they got into trouble. Not Arthur. If he fell asleep outside in the middle of winter, someone or other would always drag him in.

This man was one of the best panhandlers I ever saw. He simply had the gift of acting and he could cry at the right time. When things went wrong, Art would start singing. Now although he was from Springhill, he was no Hank Snow or Anne Murray, but he thought he was and he would milk every song for all it was worth. The tears would flow and people would say with admiration "What emotion!". It was natural therefore that the boys would egg him on and Arthur never let them down.

However finally he had had it. One year the prospect of another winter roaming the streets made Arthur desperate enough for a job. He was burning out. By pure luck we needed someone to peel vegetables and wash pots and pans. This was the beginning of a new Arthur. I say "beginning", because the boys were not about to give up on their best source of revenue without a fight. We had daily reports about Arthur's misbehaviour, about how he was smuggling booze in each day. (Cooks were not above using kitchen help as messengers for booze.) Our threat to bar Arthur from the Mission if he blew this opportunity got him into trouble with his workmates. When he told Bob the cook that he had promised me not to touch any booze or bring any into the building, Bob just laughed at him and fired him for refusing to go to the Liquor Commission. Of course the next day, Art was right back in the kitchen and he and Bob later became good friends. Or perhaps I should say, comrades in arms, since those two men spent a large part of their sober hours plotting to put one over on me. They would try anything and everything to beat me at some game, just for the fun of it. I quickly learned that the best way to get a little peace was to let everyone think that they had won the occasional battle. I could always imagine the cook saying with that French accent of his, once my back was turned, "Arr...thuur, we got the Rev that time."

~

Arthur Goes to Camp

When we eventually took the big gamble and hired men cooks for the boys' camp, Arthur went along as vegetable peeler and pot washer. There was always a sing-along after lunch and supper and the boys would clamour for the cooks, cheering like mad when they finally appeared and lined up for the singing. The first time Arthur sang for the boys, he was an instant hit and after that he managed to get involved in everything. We even have pictures of Art carrying the flag at the camp's Olympic games.

There is a story about Arthur I wouldn't have believed if I hadn't had confirmation from the federal Department of Health in Lachute. Apparently he had taken to feeding the local groundhogs, who became extremely fat with the vegetable peelings and left-overs that dear old Art served them. Art had the groundhogs trained to eat out of his hand, which was fine as long as you didn't spook the animals. Then the inevitable happened. A boy shouted in amazement when he saw Art feeding the groundhog, the animal bit Arthur, started to run away and dropped dead. Well, what an uproar. Arthur was moaning because the groundhog had bitten him and because the poor thing was dead (probably from over-eating).

Don Waite was Camp Director at the time and decided he'd better get Arthur to a doctor, so they headed off for the hospital in Lachute. After things calmed down a bit, Don took the groundhog's body back to Lachute to have it checked for rabies. Fortunately for Arthur, the results were negative.

The ribbing that Art took from then until the end of camp was unbelievable. Bob started the story that the groundhog had died from biting a poisonous Arthur. "Honest, Rev," Bob would say, in front of Arthur of course, "there was so much alcohol in Art's blood that the poor animal didn't stand a chance."

Arthur had the last laugh though. When he got home from camp, Bob gathered together all his summer savings and headed up the Main. He returned the next day still drunk and covered head to toe with lipstick: one of the ladies of the night had stolen everything while he slept.

After about five years in camp, Arthur had become a legend and was popular with everyone, not excepting the mothers. Every two weeks we would bring up a new group of campers and have a variety show in the main recreation hall to mark the occasion. Someone once had the bright idea of holding a wedding between Arthur and one of the mothers who worked in camp. According to this scenario, I was supposed to be the minister who "married" them. Of course I tried to pour cold water over that idea but somehow the plans went ahead anyway. For a variety of reasons I wasn't in camp for the show that night, so Bob Fraser, the camp's truck driver, did the honours. Apparently the wedding was a smash hit.

However it ceased to be a joke the next day when Art started asking where his wife was and why we didn't transfer her down to work with him. "What kind of an outfit is this?", he fumed. It took a while to settle him down.

I said I thought he was Roman Catholic. He allowed that he was. "And just who was the priest that married you?", I asked.

"Bob Fraser."

"And is Bob Fraser a priest?", I asked gently.

"Not likely", he replied.

"Well then, you're not married, are you?"

"Well Rev, I just felt real good, you know."

"Yes", I sympathized, "it must have been right nice." I almost said "right nice like" in the Nova Scotia jargon by mistake. He might have been tempted to throttle me: when you are around those friendly Maritime people, it's hard to resist copying them, but you'd better not get caught faking it!

~

Arthur finally had a couple of strokes and we managed to get him into a chronic care home. He used to call the front desk at the Mission at least once a week until he couldn't manage any more. One day a few years ago, I was on a radio talk show when all of a sudden I heard a familiar voice almost crying,

"God bless you, Reverend McCarthy, do you remember me?" "Of course I do, Arthur", but then he cried so much they had to close the line. Talk about a voice crying in the wilderness. It was there, still alive and I was deeply affected. The host commented that I must obviously have touched that person's life, but what I thought was, not as much as he touched mine.

Arthur was a child of God, someone with gifts he never knew how to use. Despite all his drinking, all his acting, you could see that Arthur was a good man. The Mission and its people became his family and he was loved by many people who worked or lived there.

It's tempting to say that Arthur and Bob the cook were failures, but I say to you that those fellows got their acts together as best they could and helped hundreds of men who passed through the Old Brewery Mission during the years they lived there. Like lamp-lighters, they made the world a little brighter: Arthur would relieve the pressures of life with his humour and Bob would ease the hunger for the starving crowds that came in each day.

Some people seem to think that spiritual worthiness can be measured against a pre-determined standard. Who says so? Saint Paul said "What shall we then say to these things? If God be for us, then who can be against us? Who shall lay anything to the charge of God's elect? It is God that justifieth. Who is he that condemneth? Who shall separate us from the love of Christ? Shall tribulation, or distress, or persecution, or famine, or nakedness, or peril, or sword? No, in all these things we are more than conquerors through Him that loved us." I would venture to say that St. Paul was talking about men like Arthur and Bob. It is God that justifieth and I cannot condemn them.

"God be with you 'til we meet again"

Brother Monk

During one session at the summer camp, a man I hadn't known before made quite an impression on me: he was very well-spoken in both French and English, was clean and seemed a misfit among the rest of the men at camp.

His cleanliness and fastidiousness while working in the dining room made it clear this man was not an ordinary visitor to the Mission. I wondered whether he might not have served in a religious order at one time or had even been a priest. Chatting to him a few evenings later, I discovered that he had in fact been a member of a teaching order and that his name was Raymond.

When we returned to the city, Raymond began to work full-time in the clothing department at the Mission and for the first time in many years, it was well run and clean.

Part of our agreement with Raymond was that when he had pulled himself together and had a few weeks pay in his pocket, he would rent a room outside the Mission, taking the first real step towards becoming independent again. Raymond did very well with the program until he fell ill in the second year of living on his own.

The recovery period was fairly long and Raymond was forced to retire, although he came into the Mission to visit us from time to time. He had qualified himself for Unemployment Insurance and eventually an old age pension. Then one day we had a call from the police to say that Raymond had passed away in his room. He had identified us as his next of kin. Mel Favreau and I went to the morgue to identify him and made the arrangements for his funeral and burial.

Was it possible that in Raymond's mind he had somehow disgraced himself, his Church and his family and believed there was no way back? It is difficult to explain how a very religious person could end up on skid row, but Saint Paul said, "Let him that stands take heed lest he fall."

Gibby's

The first I heard of the idea of my friends Gibby and Allan opening a restaurant in Montreal was when Allan called and said "Mac, why don't you drop by the store? We have some good news for you."

When I got there, Allan said, "We're opening a new place in Old Montreal and calling it "Gibby's". We're going to cater to big business and I'm going to set up a couple of ticker tape machines for the stock brokers at lunch. What we really want is to hear you say it won't work."

"O.K., it won't work. The high rollers are moving up to Dorchester Canyon and west; the hustlers just grab a beer and a roast beef sandwich for lunch. Anyway, the good ones I know have got short arms and deep pockets. You'll be lucky to get them to come to dinner, never mind lunch." Well, we all know why I was a skid row priest and they are successful businessmen.

Shortly after their opening and the OBM's move into the new Clark Street quarters, Gibby called. "I was talking to my partners and we thought we would like to put on a special meal at the Mission. We know that you do a big meal at Christmas, but do you have any other ones? Could we do Thanksgiving?" Of course I was delighted and every year since, Gibby or Allan has come down and helped serve the meal. Gibby's pays the going rate per plate and we cook the food and arrange to serve it in banquet form.

The Thanksgiving dinner was intended as a memorial to Gibby and Allan's father, Mr. Rosenberg (lovingly called "The Boss" when he wasn't around). The two sons remember men going in to their father's store and asking for a dime or a quarter. The Boss would say "My good man, I will do better than that. If you will sweep my floor, I will give you a dollar." He found other chores for those who came back; the men from the Mission on Inspector Street found a new friend.

When these dinners had been running about seven years, I got a phone call from the British Trade Commissioner who was moving his office to Toronto. "I have a few cases of Australian wine I think your men would enjoy." I assured him they would and we agreed that each man at the Thanksgiving dinner would have a half of glass of wine. But who could we trust with it? Gibby brought along a helper, Eddy Burns, an old catering firm operator and one of his buddies.

Eddy poured the wine that year and although a teetotaler himself, he agreed to buy the wine the next year. The following year his wife did the same, in memory of Eddy. For years afterward Mrs. Burns served in the kitchen for both the Christmas and Thanksgiving Day dinners. Today she lives in Calgary near her daughter and Gibby supplies some of his house wine.

Allan and Gibby are as different as night and day, but together they made substantial contributions to the Mission. As Mothers' Day approached one year, Gibby asked his brother to take care of getting the roses for the ladies. After some consideration, Allan said, "Gibby, anybody coming to the restaurant for dinner on Mothers' Day must have received at least a dozen roses before she even gets here. Instead, why don't we give the money we would spend on flowers to the mothers' camp at Camp Chapleau so a few needy mothers can have a happy vacation?" So another tradition was born and for over twenty years, four or five mothers have been subsidized through the Mothers' Day Flower Fund, courtesy of Gibby's Restaurant.

~

Early one December, Bishop MacLean called me to say that the Archbishop of Canterbury and the Canadian House of Bishops were coming to a meeting that summer and that the Bishops had agreed they should have a dinner at Gibby's. I was asked to find out what the cost would be and what kind of a deal could be struck.

Probably for the first time in my life, I took immediate action and called Gibby. The Bishop and I got a free lunch and he made the menu selection with Gibby's help. I thought that was the end of my involvement. Foolish me... Another call from Bishop MacLean. "Thanks, Bill, for the help in setting up the restaurant and the meal for us. Now I want you on my committee."

"You've got to be kidding!", I protested. "I never sit on committees; all they do is talk."

"You're on the committee and you'll be there for the first meeting. Give my best to Colette." *Amen.*

Along with the Bishops' meetings, I had quite a few more with Gibby. We did everything we could to make the event an outstanding success. A major item was the hospitality bar that was supposed to be supplied by one of Canada's largest distillers. After much fuss, they offered to give us four forty-ouncers of liquor — no bar, no bartender. Gibby thanked them and said that was not acceptable. We both knew Mrs. Stephenson from Corby's and we put the problem to her. She came through, providing all the drinks and the wine for the meal. She was sorry she could only provide us with a portable bar, unfortunately no bartender. That was quickly rectified when Tom Bargabello of the Piccadilly Club and his son volunteered to serve for us. (The company which had refused to support the event lost a lot of business over the next few years.)

On Christmas Day, the president of Samson Limousine was serving turkey dinners to some 500 homeless people at the Mission and asked me to let him know if there were ever any other way he could help. I didn't forget his offer. Before the Bishops' first meeting, I gave him a call, confirmed that his firm had handled the transportation for His Holiness the Pope's tour and described the requirements for the upcoming visit. "I can't possibly supply buses for the seventy Bishops, but I can provide a couple of limousines for three days with experienced drivers."

When the subject of transport came up at the meeting, the committee said it had already selected a couple of retired gentlemen with Cadillacs to do the driving, but I went ahead and suggested the limos anyway. They argued about cost, but that fizzled out because Ron had agreed to supply them for nothing.

The big day arrived and the sun shone brightly on a clear day. After some heavy persuasion, Bishop Hollis had consented to have the working committee attend the dinner. We had a table at the back and sat with the Archbishop's Chaplain and Terry Waite, who on that occasion was serving as secretary to the Archbishop and aide de camp. A few months later he was kidnapped while on a special mission for the Archbishop trying to gain the release of hostages in the Middle East. While talking with Terry at dinner and at City Hall the next day, I was very struck by his keen interest and knowledge of world events.

While desserts were being served, Gibby appeared with a souvenir menu and asked if the Archbishop would autograph it for the restaurant. The autographed menu was returned a few weeks later, accompanied by a signed picture and a note of gratitude for the wonderful food and hospitality offered by Gibby and his staff.

~

Allan and my first wife Phyllis had a favourite saying: "Some people eat to live; we live to eat". It was no surprise then that when Phyllis was a cancer patient in the Montreal General Hospital, Allan would bring food from the restaurant for her. Almost twenty years later I suffered for a couple of years with diabetes and the rich food was a no-no, so Gibby brought me tapes of one of my favourite shows, "Rumpole of the Old Bailey", for me to listen to in the hospital.

The two families shared happiness and sadness: the loss of Gibby and Allan's parents; the death of my wife, then my mother.

During the hard times, Gibby often called me up to tell me a joke. "Here is a good one for you, a man of the cloth. This guy needed some heavy money fast, so he prayed to the Lord and said "Lord, please let me win the lotto on Wednesday night." He didn't get an answer and he didn't win, so he prayed again, with the same results. Finally after four prayers and four fruitless lottos, he said "Lord, give me a break. Let me win the Lotto." This time the Lord answered: "Abie, give me a break! Meet me halfway — buy a ticket!"

It has been said that you can't pick your relatives, but you can pick your friends. When you have good ones, keep them for life. Appreciate them and never abuse them. They are like gold and will not let you down.

Brian Mulroney's handlers round up delegates at the OBM

Politicizing The Mission

While I would have enjoyed talking to a group of politicians about their indifference to the poor and homeless, I knew full well it would never happen; that's a no-win type of situation for any politician. The homeless represent less than one percent of our total population; they are politically insignificant. However, politics is a reality even on skid row. The best demonstration of that came when I least expected it.

One Friday afternoon, one of our employees asked me if it was all right to take a few of the boys to a little meeting in the Point (Pointe Saint Charles). The employee in question was a remarkable young man who happened to be between jobs. The son of a politician who was well-known on both the municipal and provincial scenes, his lively conversation made an interesting contribution to the Mission and he seemed to be doing a very good job with the men. I thought that it would make a nice Sunday outing for the men, so I said yes.

Very early next Monday morning, I received a wake-up call from the CBC newsroom in Montreal. "What have you got to say about the charges from Joe Clark's group?"

"What charges?"

"They claim that the Old Brewery Mission was involved in swinging the vote for delegates to the Conservative Party Leadership Convention."

The reporter read me the headline of the day, "Skid Row Drunks Elect Delegates for the Conservative Party" and asked me for an interview. I must confess that I have never been able to say "no comment" — even in my sleep. I asked for five minutes to prepare. With no real information, I was skating on very thin ice, but my basic premise was that the men did have a right to vote even if they lived at the Mission and that I was prepared to fight for that right. The fact that some of those men were war veterans made it an obligation to allow them to vote. Not having much to go on, I just kept affirming that the men had the right to vote anywhere, any time. Frankly, I had never been a Conservative, but I respect the right of anyone to vote.

Less than an hour later, the organizer of the expedition was in my office. I demanded to know what had happened.

"It was just that I wanted to go to Ottawa as a delegate, so I had to round up some votes. I knew how many I had but just to be sure, I talked it up with some of the old fellows upstairs. They joined the Party, so I asked them to come and vote for me.

I managed to get a loan of a school bus and brought the men to the meeting."

"So what's all the drama?"

"Well... Someone in Joe Clark's gang heard about what we were planning. They were waiting for us — with the media — when the bus started loading up with the men at the Mission."

"Beautiful", I remarked. "What's the story about the beer?"

"Do you really think our guys would go for cookies, sandwiches and petits fours, Rev? One of the boys brought out a couple of cases of beer. I swear that's all there was to it."

"Marvellous" I said. "Thanks a lot." What else could I say?

Bring on the media. They didn't seem awfully interested in perspective, insisting that there was a great scandal that was going to rock the foundations of the Conservative Party of Canada. The whole country heard about the Mission and the "bogus" voters. National television news carried the pictures of the men getting on the bus to go vote. Every daily newspaper in Canada jumped on the wagon. It was as if the whole country needed a laugh at someone else's expense; in this case that someone else was the Mission and the Conservative Party.

The selection of delegates was challenged and a hearing was held in the luxurious Bonaventure Hotel, overlooking the Old Brewery Mission a mere six blocks away. The panel was made up of real heavyweights in the Conservative Party: Senators, M.P.'s and some of the party brass. The committee was very impartial and dealt seriously with the incident. The questions were clear and to the point. The election of a new party leader could and did mean the election of a new Prime Minister of Canada; the nominations not only had to be clean but they had to look clean.

Part of the losing candidate's claim was that the men from the Mission had no valid identification: there had been a big argument at the door because one fellow had no driver's license, just some green card from an unknown association.

When I spoke at the hearing, I told the committee about the work of the Mission and gave them a little background on the men who lived there. With reference to the need to have valid identity, I mentioned that it cost close to ninety dollars to renew your driver's license in Quebec. It was ridiculous to insist that in order to vote for the Conservative Party, one was required. On the subject of the green card, I remembered that one of the men who had gone to the meeting was a member of the Korea Veterans Association of Canada. I showed my green K.V.A. membership card, which was indeed the kind of card in question, and said that if I was refused entry to a Conservative meeting on that basis, then I would certainly want nothing to do with them.

The committee was very sympathetic and even decided to visit the Mission that night, interviewing some of the men who had voted. I was amazed by the sincerity and the respect shown to the men and also by the men's very animated responses to the Senators.

The vote was upheld and our Mission driver went to the National Convention.

After the verdict was given, the boys told me that a group of patients from a chronic care hospital up the street had voted that same day for the other candidate and the votes from the Mission evened things out. The patients deigned to eat the cookies, cakes and sandwiches! What can you say? That's politics.

I Was Naked and You Clothed Me

For the want of shoe leather

In my early years at the Brewery Mission at 529 Inspector Street, keeping the men from freezing their feet at the onset of winter was a major battle — the fight to save soles. The men would slip pieces of cardboard into their shoes as linings.

Our clothing department was basically a storage and changing room with just a few racks of clothing: suits, pants, some shirts and a very few pairs of shoes. We rarely had socks or underwear. It was a big event when we bought 144 pairs of workman's woolen socks once a year. Shoes were worth their weight in gold. The only source was when someone from the family of a recently deceased man called and asked us to pick up his clothing. I remember seeing the clothing room clerk trying to remove cleats from golf shoes!

One day I received a telephone call from an elderly lady in Ville Saint Pierre asking if we had received her donation of twenty five dollars and, if so, where was her receipt? After I verified that we had not received the money, she insisted that I go out to her house and pick up a new cheque. To be honest, I tried to talk my way out of it but, ninety minutes later, I was on my way to see her and drive her to do her banking! After the chores were done, she gave me a cheque for two hundred and fifty dollars to buy winter boots for the men!

Flush with that generous gift, I called Brian McKeown, brother of a fellow priest, and asked him to hunt up some men's rubbers. So a lost cheque for $25 parleyed itself into two hundred pairs of overshoes. And so it went over a period of thirty years. Our words of motivation became: "Wait not. Go out and hustle."

A local meat packing company we had dealt with for many years decided to give us all of their used safety boots whenever new ones were bought for their employees. These boots were usually in good condition and were a big hit with the men living at the Mission, particularly during Montreal's harsh winter months.

However, the shoe jackpot came after a family broomball match: the McCarthy family vs. la famille Fortin. We lost the game but won the war. Raoul Fortin, it turned out, was both a gracious winner and the manager of a shoe company which, for several years thereafter, delivered truckloads of shoes that had been returned from their local stores across the province.

~

It paid, too, to have generous, hard-working relatives. My cousin Isobel was married to Jim Anderson, then the sales manager for Dominion Textile. Jim was able to send the Mission cases of returned sheets, towels, blankets and so on for many years and, even after he was transferred to Toronto, made sure that his successor maintained the tradition. Remember that those goods would otherwise have been sold as waste for perhaps a penny a pound. Instead they became a welcome and warming gift to the needy men at the Mission.

Several years later, I met the president of Dominion Textile and mentioned Jim, who had recently passed away. It turned out that the president was originally a Verdun boy and knew all about our work. He offered to help us in any way he could and we were happy to draw on his kindness again and again over the years.

~

At the Brewery Mission, clothing was distributed according to three categories. Ordinary, functional clothes would be issued to fellows who appeared not to care much about their appearance. It would serve no purpose to give them a good suit (actually, we never gave anyone a whole suit as they would sell it for sure). However, if a man was really trying, he would get better quality clothing. Finally, if someone was really progressing — perhaps even looking for a job — he would be given the best we had to offer. It was remarkable to see the rehab workers all dressed up on special occasions. We used to kiddingly call them bank managers. Chances are, they were wearing some bank executive's suit!

~

Many well-known Montrealers brought their used clothing to the Mission with no fanfare. Donald Gordon, my old boss at the CNR, was a Scottish immigrant who had fought his way to the top, all the while remembering just how difficult life could be. He didn't forget those he passed on the way up.

After he passed away, as per his request, we received his whole wardrobe. He was a very big man physically and we could always find someone who badly needed an oversized pair of shoes, pants or jacket. But what to do with the ten-gallon hat that had been presented to Donald Gordon by the City of Calgary? It took me two years to find a man with a head size big enough to appreciate it. When I finally did, old Nick proudly paraded around the streets of old Montreal with that stetson; in the summer, he wore it around camp, often wearing very little else. What a sight!

Clothing donations to the Mission came from far afield. For example, Marcel Poirier, the ex-chief of police in my old parish of Roxboro, was stationed at the Dollard des Ormeaux police station where he organized a Saturday depot. It was like old home day for me, many of my former parishioners and friends dropping by to donate their clothing.

From time to time, various clothing stores would hold sales, giving special discounts if you turned in your used clothing for the Old Brewery Mission.

~

By far the largest clothing collection we ever had came one winter weekend through a special event organized by CBC staffers. George Springate headed the campaign, along with David Bronstetter and Kathy Keefler. Pick-up points were arranged at several major shopping centres, all staffed by CBC personalities.

We ended up with approximately twelve tons of new and used clothing, which was great, but we had no obvious way to deal with it. Talk about being all dressed up with no place to go! The Mission had two vacant stores with 18-foot ceilings, now crammed full of clothing. How were we going to sort it all?

One of my Legion contacts told me that the Church of the Redeemer in Côte St. Paul was up for sale, so off we went to the synod office to convince a charitable Bishop's Executive Officer to look favourably upon our borrowing the deconsecrated church. Our request was a little out of the ordinary and some people might have been uneasy that we were going to fill the church with homeless people. However, the Reverend Canon Sandilands, the Executive Officer, was more than cooperative and Bishop Hollis, too, had no doubts about the issue and granted our request. Instead of paying any rent, we simply paid the heating and carried the liability insurance until they sold the church.

We had a work crew at the church every day for four or five months and two watchmen to insure no one would break in or cause any damage. My wife Colette worked there four or five days a week for months helping with the sorting.

Publicity is sometimes a two-edged sword: the Old Brewery Mission was becoming very well-known to Montrealers and the numbers of calls for help trebled. However, contributions began to increase at the same time, which made life less stressful, if not any less busy.

Organizing and distributing clothing at the Mission was sometimes a major headache. The clothing room definitely took a lot of supervision over thirty years. Many times we had to stop and start all over again. Through trial and error, we found that it was far easier and more dependable to hire an outsider to distribute the clothing than to hire a rehabilitation prospect from within the Mission. We learned early that the fellows who bought the clothing clerk beer in the local tavern often got the best clothes. The only way to stop that was to hire an outsider and bar him from drinking locally.

Christmas dinner served   *The Montreal Star*

Christmas at The Mission

Over A Century Of Tradition

When I first started helping serve Christmas dinners at the Old
Brewery Mission in 1957, the tradition was then already over
seventy years old. During those years, the Mission served
between 700 and 900 Christmas meals and followed that up with

a musical show put on by the Montreal Musicians Guild. (By the 1980's, we had lost the Montreal Musicians Guild, but the West Hill High School Band and music department took over. Although they have since had to disband, ex-students I run into still remember those times with fondness and their contribution will not be forgotten.) At the time, the OBM had just about the only open house Christmas dinner in Montreal; everything else was closed up tight. The Salvation Army always held their big dinner around the fifteenth of December to allow their religious workers to go to church on Christmas and give the staff a break. The Welcome Hall Mission served a light supper Christmas night, but by agreement with us, have had a special New Year's dinner for the last thirty years. The Sisters at Acceuil Bonneau had tried having a traditional midnight Mass followed by a party, but the boys nearly caused a riot so they decided to hold their meal at the same time as ours or even a half hour earlier. That cut our numbers considerably, but nothing was lost, because like the rest of us, the men just ate turkey sandwiches and turkey à la King for the next few days. The average number of meals served at the OBM on Christmas Day is now down to about 400.

Over the years, more and more people started to serve Christmas dinners for the poor and that was good. Even restaurant bars are now open on Christmas Day. That isn't so good: you can imagine my dismay when my ex-Assistant Director started buying a few rounds for the staff while we were trying to pull together clean-up crews after the breakfast!

For years we had to make the men line up outside in the cold to wait for the meal to be ready. However eventually the building renovations gave us two interior staircases running up five floors, so the people can now wait inside the building out of the weather. We do have to provide supervision, because these people want to use the washrooms and you cannot have 400 people wandering around the dorms.

We always had at least 100 volunteers to serve the dinner and clean up afterwards. Recently a couple of Mission Directors have taken exception to the great number of volunteers and insisted that I make some changes; it almost came down to issuing tickets for the event! Our volunteers were a very unorthodox bunch: M.P.'s and even a Cabinet Minister, bankers, lawyers and some of the biggest business men in the city served right alongside ordinary church people, legion members and Korean War Veterans. Mix that with 400 homeless people and you met the world at the Mission on Christmas Day. That was a wonderful feeling.

However, this special time made the men reflect on what they had lost and that was of course depressing for them. Then too, the meal itself was often just too rich for some of our people and they couldn't eat everything that was set out before them. That was a problem that had to be handled with delicacy and tact.

~

The final gift of the day was a package of candies, chocolate bars, an orange and an apple along with tobacco and cigarette papers or cigarettes, all in a brown paper bag and handed out as the men and women left the Mission. To the homeless and destitute people, that gift was very special.

One of Canada's wealthiest men helped serve dinner on Christmas Day at the Mission for over fifty years. One year, as he was leaving during the second serving of the meal, dressed in an old winter coat that had served him well for many years, a volunteer handed him one of the brown paper bags and wished him a Merry Christmas! While he wasn't known for having a sense of humour, he related the story to his wife. She had been trying to get him to buy a new overcoat for years. From that day on he wore the most beautiful camel hair coat I ever saw.

~

For the last ten years or so, every man who has slept at the Mission on Christmas Eve has received either a new pair of socks or woolen gloves individually wrapped. These gifts are a special donation from a family in Saint Hilaire who feel they want to do something special for the men on Christmas morning in memory of God's very special blessings to their family.

And so the tradition of Christmas has been celebrated at the Mission for 105 years and I feel very privileged to have served for 35 of those years.

Rich Man, Poor Man, Beggar Man, Thief

Not everyone is what they seem to be. You've probably heard that before, but I'd like to tell you about a classic case we had at the Mission.

In my early years there, when photographers from the Montreal Star, the Herald or the Gazette turned up to take photos of the annual Christmas dinner, they always insisted on taking a picture of a certain man who bore a resemblance to Santa Claus. The other guys at the Mission would complain.

"Did you see whose picture was in the paper today? That miserable so and so. Santa Claus, he is not. Why do they do that, Rev? That guy is a nasty mooch and he has no friends. He doesn't even live at the Mission and he gets his picture in the paper year after year."

For thirty years or more, this man showed up for the occasional meal. He never was other than greedy and nasty. I told myself that he needed the Mission, but it turned out I was a little off base. Reading the paper one morning, this headline caught my eye: Millionaire Hobo. You guessed it.

The story came to light because the police had intervened in a robbery. A young thug had assumed that this old fellow was ripe to be ripped off the first day of the month because he had just cashed his old age pension cheque. At the police station it was determined that the old fellow was indeed ready to be robbed and the proceeds would have been one hundred twenty thousand dollars, carefully tucked away in shopping bags and in his pockets! (The "millionaire" tag was just a little media hype...)

"The police convinced me that it would be much safer if I put the money in the bank", he told the reporter, who did a quick background check on the man and found that the Grey Nuns had fed and cared for him for many years at Accueil Bonneau and that they had no idea he was rich. The good sisters had nothing but good to report. Seemed like a great story in the middle of a slow week, so the editor decided it was front page material.

We were all shocked, but probably not as much the wife and two children he had abandoned fifty years earlier. The Journal de Montréal printed her story the next day and the "millionaire" of yesterday pulled a Houdini disappearing act.

Chapter Twenty

Albert

One evening there was a big fire in an apartment building in the Amherst Street area. The civic authorities arranged for Albert to be temporarily housed at the YMCA. Three days later he was told by the police that he had to find a room somewhere else, as the city would only pay for three days' accommodation. The man was very confused, so the policeman offered to bring him to the Mission. In accordance with house rules, poor old Albert had to take a shower that night, at which point I got a phone call from the night supervisor. It appeared that Albert was literally rolling in money; in fact he was wrapped in it, thirty-two thousand dollars worth. We locked it in the Mission safe.

The next day, the poor assistant manager of the CIBC was unhappy about having to count out the money before it could be destroyed (it was in pretty nasty condition). He might have been in a better mood if he had stopped to appreciate how much better off he was than poor Albert, who was by now completely lost.

In the weeks following, we learned that Albert lived the life of a city hermit because he had been incarcerated for twenty-five years in the mental wing of Bordeaux Jail, in the basement block set aside for men who were being accorded no treatment. Today he is terrified of police and people in general. When it became obvious that Albert could not function on his own and needed chronic care, friends of ours at the Heather Lodge in Rawdon agreed to take care of him. He has lived very happily there for years.

While this story ended on a reasonably positive note, the horror of this man's life couldn't be denied. Many of my associates and friends had a big hand in helping this lost soul and others like him to live happier lives. Two psychologist friends were deeply involved in closing down the black hole in Bordeaux Jail and eventually getting help for the hundreds who were locked up there. Thanks also go to the firemen who seldom get any recognition, to the policemen who had enough compassion to bring Albert to the Mission, to the night staff at the Mission who could have disappeared overnight with all of Albert's money — but didn't — and finally to our friends in Rawdon who cared for him for many years.

Because "bag people" carry everything they own in those shopping bags, they are often victimized by thugs who roam the streets looking for easy prey.

One very sad case was "The Moose". This fellow had inherited a large amount of money, which was in an account at a major trust company. Every day this poor man was forced to make a withdrawal by his companions so that the boys could drink. On many occasions he was badly beaten beforehand and would arrive at the offices still covered with blood.

We were alerted by officials at the trust company and we convinced The Moose to move into the Mission, pay room and board and let us give him a daily allowance, which was later repaid by the trust company. Since the boys on the Main could now only steal two or three dollars a day from him, they stopped taking chances with being arrested and left the poor man alone. They were no doubt afraid to take on the Mission as well.

~

Then there are the just plain greedy. An old fellow was charged with fraud, having been discovered collecting as many as seven welfare cheques a month from the Government of Quebec. Since there was no way he could deposit the money in the bank, he kept his hoard at home. His lifestyle and habits made somebody suspicious: his house was raided and the money was found in the sugar tin, the bread box and the cupboards. He went to jail for the night and then the long court process began. Due to his age and medical condition, the sentence was very light, especially since restitution was promised. The bill amounted to some thirty-two thousand dollars, payable in monthly installments of about $250 a month. The old fellow was not too happy about the arrangements and decided to appeal his case. It seems the money recovered in the raid was never turned in.

"Why should I pay back money that was stolen from me?" went his reasoning.

Anyway, while going through this process, he came to live at the Mission, paying $150 a month room and board. He spent his days in the court house across the street. After about a year, the man moved to a room outside to have some privacy. Either he found some hidden treasure or went back into business, because the debt was wiped out in about two years.

~

I was never comfortable in the role I once had to assume of probation officer. Buffalo Bill, an old-time resident, had been charged with the murder of one of his drinking partners in a flop house. The man was a 350 lb. diabetic who caught his partner stealing the group's morning bottle of wine. During the ensuing fight the man fell down two flights of stairs and died. The judge ruled that it was a drunken brawl, there had been no real intent to kill, and he sentenced Bill to two years' probation, to be served at the Old Brewery Mission under my supervision. He only had a year or so to serve, having done over six months pre-trial detention. During that time he had been alcohol-free and did well for the remaining year. When his time was up, he went back to Toronto, sober, contrite and alive. He was eating reasonably rationally, was drinking very little and his diabetes was under control. Bill was pretty lucky to shake the dust of Montreal off his heels and head back to Ontario a free man with a few dollars in his pocket. He was happy — I was relieved.

Serving a cup of coffee at Camp Chapleau   *Len Sidaway, The Gazette*

Chapter Twenty One

The Family of The Black Watch

Jimmy

Jimmy never got over the war. Like many others, his terrible experiences exacted a great toll and if you know how the famous Black Watch Regiment in particular was decimated, perhaps you can understand why many of it members — like Jimmy — found solace in the streets, alcohol and one another's friendship. Their fellow citizens classified them as weaklings, unable to control their drinking. In addition, it took the Department of Veterans Affairs a long time to understand the trauma the veterans experienced with flashbacks. By then, many of them had become addicted to alcohol and were branded as social misfits, many dying way before their time. Most were never treated for these flashbacks, so they adapted survival techniques that they had been taught in the armed forces. It was much easier than being insulted by some bureaucrat. Others were granted asylum in veterans' hospitals or government homes, wherever they could find a place.

It is disgraceful that resources for treating war veterans are now so limited. Parliamentarians and Cabinet Ministers wear "Canada Remembers" pins to mark Canadian participation in World War II, while hundreds of veterans are passing away in sub-standard conditions.

It was only when Jimmy turned fifty-five that he was eligible for a War Veterans Allowance and could move into a room and away from the misery of the streets. Thirty years of suffering and he finally got some help from the country he went to war for. The boys on the street called it the "burned-out pension", which is exactly what it was for Jimmy.

During the twenty-five or more years that I knew Jimmy, he turned his hand to everything. We had him do odd jobs around the Mission and even had him on the payroll a few times, but the lure of friends on the streets and booze was always bigger than himself. Sober, he was an immaculate person and a hard worker with a tremendous sense of humour. Drunk, he was a veritable pest.

One lunch hour I was walking down the hill from old Place d'Armes when Jimmy accosted me, which was unusual because I was with my wife and no one usually dared ask me for money when I was with someone. Jimmy must have been feeling brave that day. "Rev," he said, "all I need is a dollar for a bottle of wine. Can you loan me a dollar?"

"Are you crazy? Money for wine?"

"Aw, come on, Rev. I'll pay you back. I haven't bugged you for months," he said. "Ask Moustache, the cop — he'll tell you I always pay him back."

Well, time was against me and the pressure was on. I had just bought my wife lunch and here I was turning down a sick man. Grudgingly I reached into my pocket and came out with a two dollar bill. "Sorry, Jimmy," I said, "that's all I have and I'm not giving you two dollars."

"That's O.K., Rev, I'll give you change" and with that, he gave me four quarters. My wife howled with laughter and I was too stunned to retaliate.

Somewhere along the line, Jimmy got himself a room. The owner took over administration of Jimmy's pension until Jimmy passed away a couple of years later. I mention that because very often people in the rooming house business succeed in taking control of, and benefiting from, these poor people's money. In Jimmy's case, it was a blessing because his mind was gone at the end.

~

Larry and Tracy

Larry was another old Black Watch member. I almost said ex-member, but those guys are never "ex-"; they will forever be part of the Regiment. The Regiment is family, period.

There were only a few men on skid row with girlfriends who walked the streets and drank with them. Larry was one of them. One day Larry said to me, "Rev, I would like to get cleaned up and get a job." Boy, this was heavy duty stuff. His clothes were crumpled, dirty and stood up on their own even when he got out of them.

After the shower, shave and change of clothes, a very shaky

Larry needed a cigarette. Once he lit up, he said, "All I need now is a job." In for a penny, in for a pound, as they say.

Why not?, I thought and started my first Local Initiatives Project. Larry's job was to wash every wall in the Mission. He not only stayed sober for eight weeks but the miser in him helped him hoard his pennies. You'd think he'd buy a package of cigarettes once in a while, but not Larry. Someone might want to bum one from him.....

At the end of the eight weeks, Larry's girlfriend Tracy was released from Tanguay Prison and he asked for the day off to find a room. The next day we agreed that since the job had been temporary, it could terminate at any time, like right then and there. Tracy and Larry went off arm in arm. At a conservative estimate, the drunk lasted five days, then Larry was back on the line — broke, sick and filthy.

Because he was a good worker and in reasonable health, Larry could suffer a while, pick up the pieces and get on with his life. Tracy on the other hand was getting into poor physical shape, deaf when it suited her and with very poor eyesight.

One Christmas Eve, Tracy had to appear before the judge. It was getting late and the judge somewhat impatiently said, "What is it this time, Tracy?

"It's my glasses, my Lord," and the judge interrupted swiftly "That's your problem. Too many glasses. You'd better cut back, seeing that it's Christmas Eve. Merry Christmas, Tracy. CASE DISMISSED!"

About five years later, I was going home one Christmas Eve and there was Tracy on the corner of St. Antoine and St. Laurent. I couldn't believe it. Larry had died several years earlier and we had seen very little of Tracy since then. I got out of my car and said "Hi, Tracy."

"Who are you?"

"It's the Rev," I replied.

"Oh hi, Reverend McCarthy. I can't see much any more."

I wished her a Merry Christmas and slipped her a ten dollar bill. "Oh my God, she said, "it's ten dollars!" So maybe she wasn't colour blind.

~

THE OLD BREWERY MISSION

There were a few other Black Watch veterans I will always remember. One fellow lost his hand in action overseas. The police used to take away his claw hand when he'd been drinking, because he could and did get very violent. When the weather turned cold, he would clean up his act, get some good clothes and head to California for the winter, where his two sisters would care for him. Each year they sent him a bus or plane ticket and off he'd go.

~

One Remembrance Day, an old Sergeant sitting on the steps of the Mission introduced me to another World War II veteran. After swapping stories, it became clear in the unspoken language of war veterans that this fellow had been up to something special during the war. I later found out that he had won a DCM (Distinguished Conduct Medal) and Bar for heroism in action. All of us know the first medal could have been a fluke but two was more than luck.

I knew this fellow wasn't living at the Mission, so I asked him where he was putting up. He confessed that he didn't have anywhere right then and couldn't get into the Mission as he had had a few drinks that day. I did the only thing I could reasonably do: as a result of that encounter, our rule was changed and the veterans were no longer barred for having had a few drinks on Remembrance Day.

~

The grandson of a friend of ours became the Pipe Major of the Black Watch and the Mission did well out of the connection. Both he and his Commanding Officer worked for the Ben Weider Sports Company which had imported thousands of cases of a Hawaii fruit drink. Alas, the labels were unilingual and a few bottles a fraction of a litre short, so the Mission received all this fruit drink free, with not even a request for an income tax receipt. That wasn't the only instance of open-handedness. When Vic Chartier was Colonel of the Regiment, all leftover food from parties and training exercises was sent to the Mission by military transport.

On a black New Year's Day in 1991, when I had undergone the first operation on my legs, I woke up to see two very special visitors: Pipe Major Andy Kerr and his Corporal Drummer, resplendent in their highland dress — an instant hit in the Montreal General Hospital. All they had to do was play an Irish jig and I thought I was in heaven. What a delightful surprise and what a kind gesture!

The Black Watch is a special kind of family, one that doesn't forget its own and those who care for them.

The Penguin

Raymond (a.k.a. "Penguin") was one of the most interesting personalities ever to pass through the Mission. I can't remember just how I got to know him, but I think he was introduced to me because, like me, he was a Korean War veteran, although he belonged to the famous Royal 22ième Regiment (the Van Doos).

The origins of his nickname weren't hard to figure out. He looked like the infamous Penguin of "Batman" fame: long, slicked-down black hair, heavy dark black eyebrows and if you can believe it, a cigarette holder! And when he repeated "Quoi?" rapidly, he even sounded like a penguin.

As a young man, Raymond had every opportunity to make good, but was rather wild. Somewhere along the way, he developed a playboy attitude to life, much to the disgust of his family. While under the influence, our bon vivant signed up to go to Korea. It's perhaps too harsh to say that the Army helped him become an alcoholic, but Raymond's view was, if you were going to be killed tomorrow, then why not eat, drink and be merry today? Little did he know that the trauma of war was to affect him until his dying day.

He was a real character. We would all smile when he started off with "I'm gonna tell you something, Rev..." and then continued with some wild story. You never knew whether it was true or not, but Raymond always told these tales with such a straight face and that fantastic French-Canadian flair of his that it didn't really matter. He always finished the saga with "If you don't believe me, ask my good friend Bob Côté, the cop" (or Judge Tremblay or the Pope for that matter). He knew everyone except maybe the Pope, but his Boss knew Ray quite well.

One Spring, we had a work party go down to Killicrankie Inn in Metis Beach to help out Mr. C.B. Powell. He always paid the boys well for their work and befriended them. We were very choosy about who went with us on these excursions, but Raymond was the best cleaner and worker at the Mission and there was no question about his going. (His antics and stories during the two weeks that we were in the Gaspé would have provided enough material for three movies.) Hard work and personal cleanliness are often signs of an alcoholic trying to sober up. So it was that when you could get Raymond to stop drinking, he was the best worker you could find. Even when Raymond left the Mission, he had ladies calling almost every day to get him to do their house cleaning.

Raymond had friends. It was not beyond a certain comrade to spend time organizing search parties to bring Raymond home, in order to save his life: this friend would dry him out and get him to do some badly needed work at the Mission to help him work off some of his demons. The brotherhood of ex-soldiers has a habit of doing things like that.

Over the years we noticed that Raymond would always disappear for the winter months. Eventually we found out he was not in jail but visiting his two sisters in California!

Some might say, "We supported that?!"

But my response is, "You put a gun in that man's hands and you trained him to kill. Then he came home — torn up and mixed up — and you dared to call him a drunk."

This man was a slave to alcohol and he worked for almost every drink he had. He died of cancer in Saint Luc Hospital, essentially abandoned. We miss his light of laughter and his antics; they made our lives easier.

Into Thy hands, O Lord, we commend our brother Raymond...

Chapter Twenty Two

An Endless Array of Characters

Figaro

Figaro said that his parents had been in a German concentration camp during the war, but had survived the Holocaust, and that he was born in Paris just before the family emigrated to Canada after the war. Both parents died, leaving their hyperactive and somewhat mentally deficient son to fend for himself and wage an ongoing battle with the City of Laval, which apparently sold the family home for non-payment of taxes.

I asked him about this. "How come the Jewish Social Services never helped you? They are really top drawer people and have always cooperated with me."

"I don't want anything to do with them goniffs", he said. My alarm bells went off. Was his story for real? I never did know the whole truth.

The money left over after the sale of the house was ten or twenty thousand dollars. Even so, Figaro felt he was being robbed. He also thought that if the Jewish Social Services got their hands on the money, he would never see it because they would declare him incompetent to handle it. Further, he believed that if he ever got money from welfare, he would have to return it to the government because of getting money for the house sale. He said that was the reason he couldn't apply for welfare.

Despite the new layers of story over the years, you couldn't get away from the fact that he just craved love and attention. He was one of the first people to set up as a singer in the Metro system; he organized the first group to get official permission to perform. Well, it kept him off welfare and we were even able to give him a used tuxedo for his act. This went on for a year before he lost interest. The next thing was that he joined the actors' union and got himself a one-day job as an extra in some movie being filmed in Old Montreal. He was disgusted with the whole experience — all that waiting around and he only made a couple of bucks after paying his dues. So he closed the book on his acting career. Somebody missed the boat, because he would have been a tremendous straight man. I called him the Mission's Sad Sack.

Figaro was a real pest — like somebody's kid brother — but just a misfit, never nasty or violent. I told the staff that we had to tolerate him, make concessions and care for that lost soul. If you let him win the odd little victory once in a while, you would be rewarded with an ear-to-ear grin. It was tough to keep the bullies from controlling and beating him though. Despite the protection we worked hard at maintaining for him, it was a losing battle: in our milieu he deteriorated and had to become aggressive to defend himself against the younger, more violent types who began to seek help at the Mission.

The last time Figaro was seen, he was happily working his way through a program at another mission, trying to look very serious and official but still basically a lost orphan looking for love and a home.

Willy

Little Willy was one of our old gang from the north end of Montreal. In those days, lots of 15-yr. old kids were getting into taverns, but because he was so short and had that baby face, Willy was kept out until he was about seventeen. Unfortunately, that didn't stop his initiation to crazy drinking and eventually alcoholism.

Willy idolized the tavern big shots and became their messenger and look-out. His problem was that he was desperate to be accepted and would believe — and do — almost anything the big guys told him. He was determined to show them he was really a somebody. They all had Cadillacs? Willy would have one. Because they all drank and were big spenders, Willy would too. Financing all that was tough, and so it was that Willy graduated from shoplifting in the five-and-dime stores on Park Avenue to the big stores downtown.

While still in his twenties, Willy married a lovely girl who had no clue what kind of a hell she was getting into: a life of heavy drinking, lies and stealing. Finally she had heard enough false promises and stories and divorced him. Willy had sense enough to realize it was his fault but it was too little, too late.

Willy got into the A.A. program but he couldn't clean up his act entirely: he stopped drinking, but continued thieving. More and more of the big stores had pictures of him, so that whenever he went into a store, he was followed. Losing his wife was bad, but the bottom really fell out when he was arrested. That was when he finally started trying to put his life in order.

Having had a taste of the good times, he decided that if he was going to work, he'd do it in style. Why drive a taxi when he could drive a limousine? A friend got him a job, but somehow Willy forgot to tell the Unemployment Insurance people that he was working, so the cheques kept coming every two weeks. Some of the outstanding bills were being paid, but really it was just enough to keep the wolves from the door.

The limousine company employing Willy got the transportation contract for the Papal visit, but Willy wasn't so happy. The R.C.M.P. screened all the drivers and Willy's scam was uncovered. Now in addition to American Express, Hydro and Bell Canada, the Government was lining up to sue him. Things were going from bad to worse.

Willy managed to stay sober through this, but the past was closing in fast. The courts were reviewing outstanding criminal charges and Willy was in serious danger of going down for the count. One of the people he had sponsored at A.A. managed to get him a good lawyer and the real process of rehabilitation began. The charges were lumped together and Willy got a six-month concurrent sentence, with a warning that the next time he made a mistake, he would be looking at two years or more.

After completing the minimum sentence, he was released to a halfway house. The Director tried hard to get him a job, but little Willy wasn't too keen on the prospect. He began to hound old friends for money; he would have been back in the can if the probation service had got wind of it. Wearing my hat as the president of the halfway house, I had Willy sent over to the Mission for a job.

Willy became the most dedicated truck driver the Mission ever had. His mother's polite little boy again, he would express the Mission's gratitude and hand out a thank-you letter for the gifts of clothing or food he picked up for us. However, eventually Willy found himself in a bind. He tried to be all things to all people and wound up not doing the job that he was supposed to be doing. In fact it was becoming difficult to tie Willy down any more, he just had so many excuses and so many things to do. The time had come to sit down and talk.

During the conversation, I determined that all was not well in young Willy's world. He was working and working and not getting anywhere: the phone calls he was getting all day long were from energetic bill collectors. I also discovered that what was actually happening was that all the running around being busy was camouflage. Although he was sober, he was still looking for that big score that would make him rich. I told Willy that unless he stopped stealing, he would never make it, sober or not.

He got the message.

The Director of the halfway house found Willy a lawyer who advised him to go into bankruptcy and start all over again. The Government agreed to monthly payments and within two years, Willy was free of debt and working happily for the Mission. A few years later, he chucked the job with us and today he is delivering flowers on a part-time basis. When he came to the hospital during my couple of years of illness, I would hear a cheerful "Hi, Rev! It's me — Willy. Don't forget, one day at a time."

Willy reminds me of the words of the old hymn by William Walsham Howe:

We give thee but thine own, whate'er that gift may be:
All that we have is thine alone, a trust, O Lord from thee...

And we believe thy word, though dim or faith may be:
Whate'er for thine we do, O Lord, we do it unto thee.

~

Also Known As...

Jack Whelan was one of our residents who ran the clothing department, the fumigator and the whole annex building on

Inspector Street. In fact anything you wanted done, Jack would find a way to do it for you. When I was first at the Old Brewery Mission, I was working late one night and wanted something to eat. All of the local restaurants were closed, but I knew from my old days in the CNR that the Windsor Tavern had good food, better by far than what was served at the local lunch counter. When I went in, there was my friend Jack, installed where he could see everything that was going on. Within ten minutes, my table was loaded with beer, thanks to ex-residents of the Mission who might need a favour one day. Most of them didn't know me, so I assumed that if you were o.k. by Jack, you were o.k. with the boys at the Mission. He sure did well that night because I refused to break my personal rule of never taking more than one drink with a parishioner. Jack didn't complain about the unsolicited pints I left for him, but the experience kept me from ever going into a tavern anywhere near the Mission for the next thirty years.

About 10 or 15 years later, Jack had a personal problem he wanted to see me about. He had just returned from sick leave and was pretty nervous; you could always tell with Jack because he needed a towel to wipe the perspiration from his face. "Bill, I don't know how to tell you this, but here goes..... My name is not Jack Whelan", he said. "I changed it when I left my wife behind in Newfoundland. During the war, she was running around with my friend, believe it or not. I still thought we could settle down after the war, but it didn't work. I couldn't apply for an army pension before now because she would have got into the act. I have been living with this girl, Ann, for five years now. I would like to pull everything together and make sure she's taken care of if something happens to me."

We made contact with our friends in Veterans Affairs and got Jack's Social Insurance Number corrected along with his Quebec Hospital Insurance card. Jack managed to retire with a war veteran's allowance and his newly adjusted Quebec Pension Fund.

Jack passed away a few weeks after my first wife died and although I had refused to take any funerals for a while, I just couldn't say no to someone who had been so loyal to me and the Mission.

~

Harry was another Mission resident, but quite different from Jack. First of all he was very reclusive and had come to Montreal from Cape Breton around the end of World War II. I am convinced that Harry was harassed as the village idiot when he was young. He probably left home packed full of hurt and hatred — or maybe he ran away from a hospital. You could see that there was lots of frustration and anger in him.

Harry worked for local grocery stores as a delivery boy for many years. However, as each store expanded, they changed over to delivery trucks and Harry lost his job each time. During the first year I worked at the Mission, he asked me for any kind of work that would keep him off the streets. Harry became the best cleaner-attendant-bed maker we ever had at the Mission. His floor was immaculate every day by noon hour. The Lord Bishop of Montreal came to visit us one day and I gave him the grand tour. When we got to the third floor, there was Harry nonchalantly looking at nothing in particular. His beds were all made and his floor was clean: you could pretty much count on that. However, you could never tell what he was going to say (if he spoke at all). Many times I'd say "Hi, Harry!" and he'd look right past me, so this time I decided not to say anything or even to introduce him. Two hours later he smashed all 14 of the 5' by 4' windows on the floor. When they got to him, he was shouting, "Won't talk to me? I'll show you!"

We got him into the Allen Memorial Hospital thanks to the Montreal Police. Ten days later he was rated non-violent and released with the proverbial bag of pills. There was no way we could employ him after that, but since he had been with us for about 20 years, we couldn't turn him out.

In order to get Harry welfare until he could qualify for the Old Age Pension, we needed to get his birth certificate from Nova Scotia. He helped us fill out the request, gave the name of his home parish — the whole nine yards, as they say. About a month later, the money order and request were returned with

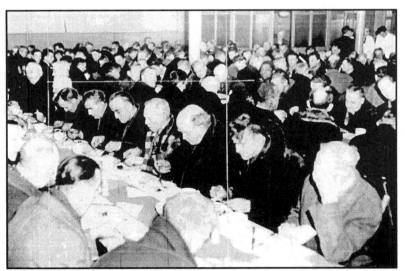

Serving dinner at the OBM, in the 1940s   *The Montreal Star*

a note that there was no record of the birth of anyone by that name during a period of ten years from the date we gave. We thought that was the last thing Harry needed to hear. We all guessed that he was an illegitimate child and how do you tell a sixty year old man that? I won't forget the words of the staff, "Rev, you are good at that kind of thing". Right. Thanks.

"Harry, we have a problem. They say in Nova Scotia that they have no record of a Harry MacBain born in Sydney Mines around that time."

"I could have told you that", he replied scornfully. "My real name is James White." I should have known.

We received the birth certificate ten days later and James White went on welfare until he received his Old Age Pension. He still lives at the Old Brewery Mission and is in failing health. A good friend of the Mission who was a psychiatrist examined Harry/James and told me that he was going to die from the disorder he had, but as the Mission was home for him, he should be allowed to stay with us. And stay with us he did.

~

THE OLD BREWERY MISSION

Porgie

Porgie was one of the flightiest people I have ever met; "hyper-active" would be an understatement. He was a human scarecrow with flashing eyes, the worst outfits you could imagine and in later years, a beard that grew in bunches all over the place. But I don't want to give you the wrong impression: Porgie may have been lacking in some respects, but he could also be brilliant. Porgie spoke with alarming speed, probably from having had his ears constantly boxed as a child. He was grateful for everything you did for him, whether it was feeding him or just listening to him without hitting him.

As a youngster in the early 1940's, Porgie attended church and Sunday School on a regular basis in the Park Extension district of Montreal, so it was natural for him to drop into local churches when he took to wandering the streets in later years. If the food and coffee were good, so much the better. He was well-liked everywhere.

One year when I was attending the annual Synod Meetings in Montreal, a delegate from one of the downtown Montreal churches talked to me about "that delightful little character from the Mission". Of course he was describing the one and only Porgie. Some Anglican churches can be more than a little English in tradition and language and this minister was from one of them. He was a really nice person, but very proper and precise — complete with an accent from across the pond.

"Porgie signed our visitors' book as Porgie Beef, OBM. Does he really have a title of some sort?", the poor man asked. It was a reasonable question, I suppose, but I couldn't stop myself breaking out into a smile.

"His Order is the OBM... Old Brewery Mission," I replied. "It seems very natural to him to sign that way."

~

Saint Michael's Mission started up many years ago in a downtown Anglo-Catholic parish. After many problems with financing and administration, the Mission got a new director, Harold Parsons, a bona fide street worker who made his mark as a very caring individual, pushing, shoving, cleaning and cooking for the Mission until it became a real hands-on agency of the church. Porgie was befriended by this friend of the friendless.

Unfortunately Harold died suddenly at a young age. The funeral in his home parish, the Church of the Advent in Westmount, was well-attended. We were halfway through the Requiem Mass when Porgie got up and stood beside the casket. I wondered in alarm what he was going to do, but in fact, he just stood there. I walked over to him.

"I didn't do any harm, Reverend McCarthy", he said, "I didn't do any harm, did I?"

"No", I whispered, "you were just beautiful, Porgie. Come and sit with me." and he did. Somewhere in the church a voice said, "Good old Porgie."

~

Summer camp was a challenge for all of us but for Porgie, it was just a bit more difficult. If someone bothered him in the city, he could just disappear, but in camp there was nowhere much to hide. When anybody set Porgie off, he would walk into the village, say he was lost and someone would drive him back to camp. He became known around town.

One day Porgie disappeared and didn't show up for supper. Search parties went out on three country roads and the boss ran out of gas hunting for him. I headed for the gas station in Morin Heights and when I got there, the first thing I saw was the town's police cruiser with the Chief himself inside. As I walked over to tell him about Porgie, he got out.

"Rev, look who I got here!"

I don't need to tell you who was sitting there looking up at me with an impish grin. Our truant said, "Sorry, Rev, I got lost. I just couldn't stop walking."

Naturally I was angry, but nonetheless relieved to see him. On the way back to camp I threatened to put him on a raft all day in the middle of the lake, but he promised to be good.

That year turned out to be tough for Porgie because his best friend Bobby died, leaving a big hole in his life. He left the Mission that fall and the next time I saw him was on the cover of a fundraising campaign folder for another mission.

I know what he would have said. "Did you see my picture, Reverend McCarthy? That was real nice, eh?"

~

Louis

Louis was a World War II veteran and a Gamma-type alcoholic — a "rubbie", someone who drank a brew made of rubbing alcohol.

One night Louis found himself without a place to sleep and nothing to drink, so he made his way to the Queen Mary Veterans Hospital, which was a long way from downtown. Arriving at the emergency clinic, he had to wait until the duty doctor could be retrieved from one of the wards. This allowed Louis to liberate a bottle of rubbing alcohol before being escorted out of the hospital by the commissionaires who had their hands full trying to quieten him down. The police were called, took Louis down to the Salvation Army Men's Hostel, but were unable to get him a bed. On the way back to the station with him, they decided that they had already spent too much time on the case and anyway, a judge would probably just release him in the morning. So they let Louis go in the next station's territory, thus saving themselves a lot of paperwork.

As it turned out, the paperwork took months to complete and the next day's headlines were "hot": Louis was run over and killed by a VIP on a main road.

The uproar in the press was considerable. This poor, defenseless, homeless man died and someone had to pay. An unusually large press contingent came to a Kiwanis luncheon I was speaking at, although it was probably the free lunch that brought them and not the speaker. They were surprised that my theme was not the horrible accident but the everyday work of the Mission. One young lady asked me what I thought of Louis' death. I said it seemed like just an accident. Louis had a blood alcohol count of huge proportions; a few more one-hundreds of a percent and he would have been dead, not just comatose.

The girl shouted "Then Louis died for nothing!" Her position seemed to be that Louis had died for a cause.

In Montreal there is a good group of excellent journalists.

Lily Tasso from La Presse came to the Mission and found out that Louis had a history of flopping in front of cars to extort money from unsuspecting motorists. That was the closest anyone ever came to the truth.

~

Billy

The very first death on the Ville Marie Expressway was of a man from the Mission. Billy was a native Indian, as he would say, and was rightfully proud of it. He appeared to have a good education with polished speech in both French and English. It was a pleasure to talk to him in his sober moments, but give him a couple of drinks and he was completely different.

Like two or three other war veterans, Billy had a steel plate in his head and the cold winter and fights he got into didn't help matters any. On more than one occasion I saw him sitting on a bench in the Mission's lobby, rocking back and forth and hitting his head against the wall, trying to get some relief from the pain. No matter what you said, the anger and frustration continued to pour out, so it was better not to say anything.

Alcoholics have you at a disadvantage because you never know where they are coming from. One day Billy was sitting in the lobby, sober and all cleaned up.

"Hey, Rev! Do you know what OBM means?"

"Everyone knows that, Billy. It means the Old Brewery Mission."

Billy shot back with "Nope, it means Old Bill McCarthy's place! Gotcha that time, Rev, I really gotcha," he yelled, roaring with laughter and running out the front door.

Unfortunately that's not how I remember Billy. One day the police and fire units were parked out front: they had found a body at the bottom of the pit where the Place d'Armes Metro station was being built. As they lifted it out on a crane-held sling, poor Billy's body just dangled in the air. It was a horrible sight that I cannot forget. He had gone behind the construction barrier to drink a bottle of wine. The luxury of that quiet drink by himself cost him his life.

~

One night there was a fire in the Mission's fumigator and a resident was found dead inside it. The police were asking all kind of questions; they originally suspected that the lad had been locked in the fumigation room and that a felony had been committed.

During that long night we were able to determine that the clothing caught fire because someone had left a Bic lighter in his jacket pocket when he put his clothes in the fumigator. The machine was like a huge clothes drier that could destroy lice and other vermin in a matter of minutes. It could also explode cigarette lighters.

The night clerk had given the dead man a break that evening by letting him into the building severely intoxicated. When the smoke was discovered and the alarm bells were ringing, someone heard him say he would take care of the problem. He disappeared into the change room and lost his life.

Our original architect, Mr. Francis Nobbs, devised a new fumigator and we built it on the top floor where, if the new extinguisher system failed, a fan would move the smoke directly out the roof vent. While the inquest completely exonerated the Mission, we felt an obligation to make the building as safe as possible, the more so when we found out that some of the people who came to us from Dernier Recours were arsonists. They did in fact start some small fires, but the alarm systems worked and the preventative measures stood the test.

~

There were many times we had to send someone to the morgue to identify people and because of the work we were doing, if the next of kin were unknown, the Mission was often granted permission to bury the man. The OBM has a few plots at the Hawthorndale cemetery which we used from time to time for itinerant men who had no relatives. The City still has "Paupers Graves", but we try to avoid that and have managed in one way or the other to provide a Christian burial for the men who die at the Mission or who are well-known to us and died alone.

Chapter Twenty Three

Volunteers from Bishop's University give The Rev a hand

Without Whose Help...

If no one had ever confronted the public with the terrible situation of the homeless in Montreal, we would be in a terrible state today. Absolutely no progress would have been made without the efforts of Soeur Monique, Marie Audet and André Jacob; we are now able to care for three or four times the number of people we served before they came on the scene.

~

Good Sisters of the Grey Nuns (Les soeurs grises)

There is no question that the Sisters had a big impact on social work in the City of Montreal, as they continued the work begun at the founding of Montreal by Soeur Marguerite d' Youville and we had the good fortune to work alongside some very special nuns over the years. But there was one little Sister who drove for Accueil Bonneau who was a special delight to us. Whenever she picked up more fresh food than they could use, Sister would bring cases of food to us at the OBM, then on to other missions. From then on, we began sharing with each other whenever we got a big load of food. We would call around and see who needed to share in the wealth. Not too long after that breakthrough, Montreal Harvest came on the scene and it and the food banks that sprang up have been a real Godsend to all of us who feed the poor.

Mel Favreau found out the Sister loved baseball, so every once in a while, he would give her a couple of tickets to an Expos game — at his own expense — because he too was mesmerized by her vim and vigour. We believe that her religious community wouldn't let her drive after her seventy-fifth birthday and sent her off to the Mother House. We really missed her.

~

Another very hard-working sister was Sister Dolores, a very intelligent and effective organizer. Sister Dolores was instrumental in building up Réseau d'aide, a support network for all agencies that dealt with homeless people just at the time the City was preparing for the 1976 Olympic Games. Throughout the year of Expo '67, the police rounded up vagrants and itinerants and people with no fixed address were given six months in jail, just to ensure that visitors would go away with a good opinion of Montreal. The first project Réseau d'aide undertook was to ensure that this terrible injustice would not recur in 1976. It did not.

The first major independent detoxification centre for homeless alcoholics was opened in the old Murling Centre on Préfontaine near Rachel, not too far from the Olympic Stadium. Sister Delores did a lot of negotiating to get that project under way and it is still operating today.

~

A very real champion of the homeless over the years has been Sister Côté. After almost a lifetime of service at Accueil

Bonneau, the good and very gentle Sister helped countless chronic alcoholics get back on their feet and turn their lives around. The idea caught on and the religious community got more involved. Accueil Bonneau, which had basically been a soup kitchen for almost a hundred years, now gave front-line treatment in various forms, such as reconstructing the Montreal Sailors' Institute into a lodging house for the home-less named Port Royal and providing the leadership necessary to run the group. I am very sure that the good Sister has over-shot the retirement mark, but she walks where angels fear to tread. She has been deeply involved in Nazareth House which looks after otherwise unwanted AIDS patients who are virtu-ally on their death beds. Sister Côté has a quiet, personal cru-sade to ensure Christian burial for anyone who dies alone, with special emphasis on the men at the missions, Accueil Bonneau and Maison du Père. The local undertakers run when they see her coming, but they all cave in under the weight of her deep empathy for a child of God who managed to get lost somewhere along the way. We have been blessed to have shared with this wonderful servant of Our Lord. She has left an indelible mark on us all.

~

One other Sister I especially remember. Soeur Monique Picard came to our attention through her efforts to find rooms for men of no fixed address who frequented Accueil Bonneau. She got to know most of the men by their first names and did a good job of keeping them in line.

At the time, there was no way a person could get welfare if they had no fixed address, but after a long, hard battle, Soeur Monique found a loophole — or maybe she even created one! A person with a receipt for a room (minimum of ten dollars) would qualify for welfare. Eventually the Government agreed to advance the down-payment in cash and when the receipt was brought back, the official application was accepted. Back and forth the Sister went with men looking for help.

Some projects worked out, others didn't. Eventually the Port Royal project got under way and Soeur Monique was put in charge of it. But not for long, for she was called to assist the Director of the new la Maison du Père, the first Francophone mission to the homeless in Montreal. With the Director's attention on the construction and fund-raising, someone was needed to care for the men and Soeur Monique was right at home with many of the people she had helped over the years.

Just about that time, Soeur Monique Picard was awarded the Order of Canada for her outstanding work with the poor and homeless of Montreal. This was truly a well-deserved honour. However, resting on her laurels was not her style and with much persuasion and a promise of help from me, she graciously agreed to be the President of Dernier Recours Montréal. The truth was she needed much more than help from me, but we managed to get her the support she needed for the task ahead. She met all opposition head on. Because of the daily confrontations at DRM, the news media were always present and while Soeur Monique gave the Director and her assistant their proper independence, she was always ready to take the flak and fight back.

A year after the closing of Dernier Recours, Soeur was running just about everything at la Maison du Père, but it seems all that fighting and serving took its toll because we heard soon after that she was on a year's sabbatical.

~

A few months before we were due to start rebuilding the Mission in 1989, I heard from a Legion friend, Colonel Bart Mallott. "Padre, could you use some metal bunks for your summer camp?" Naturally I said yes and he told me that he was consulting for a Montreal shipping company that was in the process of converting a ship into a barge. The whole stern section was being re-designed and rebuilt. He drove me to see the ship and casually let drop an offer to take any of the kitchen equipment we wanted. So to our amazement, about $40,000 of wall-to-wall stainless steel kitchen — three large refrigerators, a freezer, stoves, counters and other fittings — had dropped in our lap! The one condition was that we had exactly 48 hours to remove it.

This was a pretty problem. How do you get that kind of heavy equipment off a ship that sits thirty feet above the dock? By chance Jimmy Wilkinson, a very old Masonic friend, was removing the asbestos insulation from the same ship. He arranged with the crane operator to put in some overtime and move the equipment to our truck below. It cost us a total of $200, less than it would have set us back just getting the crane to the ship in the first place. I never regretted being a Mason, Shriner or Legionnaire; you could always find help when you needed it.

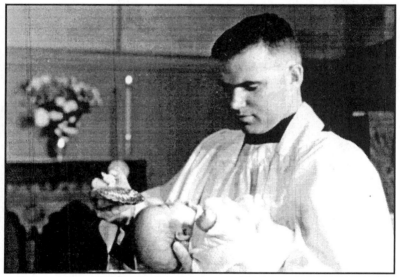

A young Rev. McCarthy baptizing a child at St. Barnabas church

My link with the Irish community was no coincidence of course, but the connection sure opened the door to a lot of good people. Liam Daly is a retired advertising executive who is one of the hosts of the Montreal Irish show on cable television. Liam never failed to have us on his show in time for our annual fundraising campaigns and any other time he could work us in, specially around St. Patrick's Day.

Liam was a quiet inspiration to me, a kind and gentle man who believed fervently in mankind, his church and his country and who prayed hard for a peaceful Ireland. You could always expect a phone call from this delightful person when things were going wrong and you needed a boost. After listening carefully to my moaning he would say, "Ah, we are but instruments of God's grace and you are certainly a gifted instrument". Somehow his words always took away the sting of my problems. Our world was richer for the experience of sharing with people like that.

I would never forgive myself if I did not say how proud I was to be named Montreal's Irishman of the Year some years back and then later, Grand Marshal of the St. Patrick's Day parade. They were unbelievable honours. Many, many friendships resulted from those experiences: the Erin Sports Association, the United Irish, the St. Patrick's Society and my beloved Irish Protestant Benevolent Society. The donation spinoffs were remarkable and amounted to thousands of dollars each year.

Jimmy Barriere was a member of the Erin Sports Association and he wanted to do something special for the Mission. His business was doing well and he wanted to give something back to society. His partner Ron organized a special fiftieth birthday party and a golf tournament to kick off the James Barriere Foundation. The Old Brewery Mission was the first recipient of $5,000. Each year Jimmy sponsored the annual variety show at the men's summer camp and made sure that his firm supplied at least ten Christmas baskets for poor camp families. Give and it shall be given unto you. Thanks, Jimmy and may God bless you.

The Irish Protestant Benevolent Society has been a strong supporter of the work of the Mission for years and they have taken it upon themselves to serve a roast beef dinner on Saint Patrick's Day each year as an extra project.

But there were other connections, too. The German Benevolent Society was the first to give the proceeds of its annual Ball to the Mission. The St. Andrew's Society followed suit and then the St. Patrick's Society.

~

The late J. Louis Levesque was the best friend and supporter anyone could ever want. He was the biggest annual contrib-
utor to the Mission for years, but he was also extremely kind to
the Mission priest, inviting him to many prestigious events,
including dinner at Rideau Hall with the Governor General.
What a thrill to be taken from the Mission to the splendour and
elegance of those great dinners. This was a tremendous boost
for my wife and me. Mr. Levesque always made sure that some
of his closest friends sat with us so that we were made to feel
welcome. He used to say, "I like what you are doing down there
at the Mission. Keep a bed for me, Father." The Old Brewery
Mission and the McCarthy family were blessed to have a good
friend like J. Louis Levesque.

One night we were on our way to one of these special awards
dinners at the Ritz Carleton; we were cutting the things close and
my wife hated to be late. She said, "Are you sure of the time?"

I snapped back, "Of course I'm sure! Here — read the invita-
tion." Oh, dear. We were a week early. So who said I was always
late? After that, how could I begrudge my wife the cost of the
elegant meal in the classy restaurant I took her to as penance?

The sequel was almost as expensive. The next week we
arrived early and my wife refused to go upstairs right away —
it would look as if we were cheap — so we went to the bar at
the Ritz. The price of a drink was about five times the cost of a
drink at the Legion. What price success!

~

Things have changed for the better. There is an awareness of the
need for help thanks to the courage and tenacity of all agencies in
the field, but a special vote of thanks goes to the people who
showed the Dernier Recours experience for what it was: a strik-
ing symbol of a population that was beginning to hide from itself.

Since the Year of the Homeless, the press has never really
been properly recognized for the dramatic part it played in
bringing home to Montrealers and the rest of Canada the desperate plight of the homeless and destitute people in our city.
Preachers sermonized, social workers cried, social scientists
made charts and psychiatrists and politicians wove fancy sto-

ries, but the damned ugly facts of life on our streets were nowhere as vividly brought home to us all as in the local and national media.

In order to give a proper tribute to the forces working to improve the lot of the homeless in those most difficult years, a whole book of recognition should be written. Mayor Jean Doré showed the way and opened the purse strings. City of Montreal Executive Chairman, John Gardiner, then his successor Madame Lea Cousineau, withstood tremendous pressure from others who wanted to kill the Dernier Recours project. Our requests to Marc-Yvan Côté, the Minister of Social Affairs for Quebec, never fell on deaf ears. The specialists in housing at SDHM (Société d' habitation Montréal) and the SHQ (Société d' habitation Québec) time and time again came to our rescue, especially with the acquisition of the building at 6400 Clark St., which is now named Maison Roger Beaulieu in honour of our late vice-president.

Throughout all of this, the OBM actually tripled its services to the needy, not just of Montreal, but of Quebec; many rural people moved into the city during those years, along with hundreds of immigrants who had no other place to stay.

Michel Plante, our architect, and his colleague Claude Marrie knew how to navigate through the City departments we needed help from and also made introductions that saved us of a lot of time, going with hat in hand on our behalf. Costs nearly got away from us but we had a backup architect watching the game very closely and Roger Beaulieu carrying the big stick for us.

We could never relax: the Government was very slow making its payments, the contractors demanded their money on time and the rate for overdrafts was 18% then. We were looking at big losses due to bureaucratic delays. Having Mr. Daniel Johnson of the Quebec Treasury (later Premier of Quebec) as guest of honour at the official opening really straightened that out for us. The Board of Directors were behind us all the way and without that encouragement and their fund-raising activities, we would not have been anywhere near as successful.

People looking for grants must realize that financing is a very serious problem; it will create major headaches for you unless you make the proper banking arrangements and keep from getting tied up in overdrafts. We were very fortunate that we did not. I know of other associations who lost everything because they simply assumed the Government would pay its bills on time. There is tremendous joy in receiving a grant for a million dollars, but make sure of the conditions when applying and double-check before signing on the dotted line. People only fool themselves when they say they don't need legal advice. We at the Old Brewery Mission were blessed with the support, advice and loving care of the late Roger Beaulieu throughout his many years at the Mission. Leadership of that calibre isn't easy to find, but there are many people of that stature who are just waiting to be asked to lend a hand. Missions should look outward from time to time.

~

Martha

We first met Martha at Camp Chapleau, where she was helping out in one of our three kitchens. My wife Phyllis was finding our six-month old son Earle a big handful, so we were in the market for a cleaning lady to help out once a week. (What a joke! For years afterward, it was "I've got to clean up the house — Martha's coming tomorrow.") Martha was good company for Phyllis and helped us out a great deal while Phyllis was sick with cancer. She always had a store of tales to brighten up the day.

Although a resident of Montreal for a good fifty years, Martha never lost the glorious Scottish accent she had when she stepped off the boat from the auld country. She had a wonderful sense of humour, but those whiplash comebacks of hers stung. You had to be on your toes if you wanted to keep up with her and as we got to know her, we learned a few tricks so we could hold our ground with her. One fairly effective tactic was to say "Slow down, Martha. I didn't understand you. What did you say? And say it in English please." Then while she caught her breath and repeated the story, we could be preparing our repartee — at least that gave us half a chance.

Martha had at least ten adult children. Some were thirty years old acting like sixteen and most of the boys did time in prison. Mind you, according to their mother, it never was their fault — the police blamed them but they didn't do it. On at least three occasions, I had to go across to the court house and post bail. Some of my Roman Catholic clergy friends told me later that they had to do the same from time to time. The daughters' romances were an open book at our house, but you couldn't believe half the stories. None of it mattered to Martha. As far as she was concerned, her children could do no wrong. As long as there is life in this tired body of mine, she seemed to say, I will fight for them. And fight she did.

The children made unreasonable demands on the good will of their mother. Once she was looking for a typewriter for the son who was doing time in the pen. Phyllis suggested I could do Martha a favour at very little cost by getting a used typewriter in one of the pawn shops on Craig Street. My reaction was that that fool son of hers was too stupid to even be a crook, let alone a student or writer. I knew that typewriter was merely going to be a status symbol in the cell block and the next thing we knew he'd be asking for gold cuff links or even some hash. Sure enough, the guards intercepted a package of hash-filled cigarettes carried in by — you guessed it — his dear old mum.

It wouldn't be fair to blame the sons and daughters entirely because Martha really spoiled them. But her biggest gift to them was that she taught them how to survive.

During Phyllis' prolonged illness, Martha faithfully came to our house once a week and reported back to Phyllis in the hospital. On another day in the week, Martha would help my mother-in-law (Nanny Burgess), more to give her spirits a lift than anything else: Phyllis was her only child and her husband had died a couple of years earlier. A few months after Phyllis passed away, Martha called me to say that something seemed wrong with Nanny, so I came and took her to Emergency at the Montreal General Hospital. She soon talked her way out of there. Her daughter had just spent the best part of four years as a patient in that hospital and she wanted to go home. I convinced her to come to my house, where she had a stroke the next morning. Once again my thanks were owing to Martha — Nanny could never have never made it to the telephone if she had been home alone.

Just over a year later, my own mother was diagnosed with advanced cancer. Once again Martha stepped into the breach. We moved my mother in with us, Martha dropped her other customers and came to the house five days a week.

During that time, my second wife Colette and I had to go to Chicoutimi to attend the funeral of her brother-in-law. After we arrived, we called to make sure that everything was all right. My sister assured me that all was well, but that we might have a problem when we got back — Martha had just won $45,000 in the Lotto 6/36! Fortunately she took $5,000 in cash and put the rest in 90-day term deposits. She missed a total of one day caring for my mother and then only because she wanted to do the banking herself for fear that her beloved husband Liam might do something foolish with the money. She stuck with us until Mum went into the hospital for the last time.

One day I got a call that Martha had had a massive heart attack and was in the hospital. She didn't make it through the night. The funeral home was full for the wake, people coming from near and far to share the sad time with the family. When Earle and I got to Saint Anthony's church for the funeral, I said we would wait until everyone had gone in, as I just wanted to spend the service praying for Martha and Phyllis. However, after a few minutes I thought we had better go and see what was wrong, since things were late getting started.

Late because they were waiting for me, as it turned out. Father O'Rourke told me that the family wanted me to take part of the service. Having read the Epistle in many French and English Roman Catholic churches, I felt quite at ease doing that, but supposed the celebrant would read the Gospel.

"You will read both," he said. "Come into the sacristy and get robed."

So I read the Epistle and Holy Gospel and then sat back to listen to a very inspiring sermon on Life, Death and the Resurrection. I nearly fell off my seat when he talked about Martha and particularly her love of her children, her deep faith in the church and her tenacity. Martha would reach out and grab you, he said, and she wouldn't let up until she got the help she needed for her children.

"One night she got me out of bed," said Father O'Rourke, "to go down to the police station to get her son out. Then the next day I had to go in front of the judge to beg for leniency — and it worked!" So the good Father and I had more in common than I had realized.

Father O'Rourke and I celebrated the Holy Eucharist together, sharing the Body and Blood of Our Blessed Lord. What an experience — I was shaking. I had never, ever anticipated doing that in a Roman Catholic Church and I looked up to the heavens and said " Martha and Phyllis, you really got me that time".

The Warden of the Church Of the Advent was at the service and said, "What will your boss Bishop Hollis say when I tell him about this tomorrow?"

"Probably not as much as Bishop Crowley will when he gets his hands on me."

But I am sure Our Blessed Lord was smiling and saying "I told you guys that it would work. Anglicans and Roman Catholics can, should and will get along together in my Name because it is the will of My Father."

Martha helped me and mine. I helped her and hers and He helped all of us. *Requiescat in pace*

~

And The Church Was There

Well-meaning letters to the editor asking why we don't open our churches to the homeless infuriate me. Worse, we never see any reply from the clergy. The answer is simple enough: churches are places of worship set aside for prayer and meditation, consecrated and blessed so that people may go there to contemplate the infinite majesty and glory of God, the Father. But when people see no response from the Church, it looks as though it just doesn't care.

It would be a gross exaggeration to say that all homeless people are harmless victims of society. What we saw going down at

Chapter Twenty Three

Rev. McCarthy delivering a sermon in the 1980s

Sanguinet Street brought that home to all of us. Drugs, sex and violence were the order of the day in that milieu. Dragging that into churches would have been disaster and you can't convince me otherwise. Yes, the Christian Church has a responsibility to provide care and lodging for the poor. Yes, churches are open for public and private worship, but you must not profane or blaspheme those churches by allowing the wanton use of them.

In my mind there are two ways to think about the Church: the formal and the unorganized. Both are part of the Body of Christ. Like the organized Church, the informal part also draws its strength and traditions from Holy Mother Church and responds to the command of our Blessed Lord to "Feed my sheep". This it does in many ways. What we did at the OBM was to create a special mission to help raise people up from the misery they found themselves in.

In the last days of the twentieth century, more and more people are joining the ranks of the informal church, responding to the call for social action, and drawing away from the organized churches. These are people who want to be able to answer these questions to the satisfaction of their hearts:

I was hungry — did you feed me?
I was sick — did you comfort me?
I had no job — did you help me find work?
I was in prison — did you visit me?
I needed your prayers — did you pray for me?

These are the cries of the poor and suffering and inasmuch as we do nothing, we do nothing for Christ. Fortunately many practicing believers did what they had to do in their own way to assist the write-offs of our church and society. These people came from all walks of life, rich and poor, professionals and ordinary working people. Very few wanted any recognition, they just wanted to do something.

~

I would be very remiss if I did not acknowledge the support of my Bishops, who were my true spiritual Fathers in God. Not only did they put up with me, they really supported me over thirty-five years: Archbishop Dixon; then Bishop Maguire and Archbishop Hollis, who suffered the most with me, but was a true friend; Bishop MacLean, my old parish priest and good friend; and last, but surely not least, Bishop Hutchison, who faithfully sat through close to three hours of sermons on the Last Words of Christ one Good Friday. The support and friendship from him and his wife Lois were greatly appreciated during my prolonged illness. The fellowship of many priests in our diocese and hundreds of laymen provided strength that helped me through. I must mention the Reverend Doctors R.L.S. Slater and Eric Jay, the two principals at the Montreal Diocesan Theological College who gave me support, inspiration and much needed personal discipline.

The late Bishop Allan Goodings of Quebec was an old school-mate, fellow football player and confidant. He worked one summer at the Mission and lived to talk long and hard about it. While in college Bishop Goodings was a bit of a rough diamond. He had been working at Canadian Vickers as a ship's engineer and some of that environment's less-than-gentle style of speaking often came out. One Monday morning at school, Allan was the student in charge of piling the sheets and pillowcases from each room for the cleaning ladies, so that they could be counted and sent to the laundry. (It was too early for the ladies to go into the seminarians' rooms, so the students had to take turns getting the laundry together.) Being somewhat frustrated by the extremely slow response from his fellow students, Allan began to shout and hammer on doors.

"Come on, you guys! Get your dirty sheets out here. What do you think this is?"

Out from his room stepped our unflappable Cambridge exchange student, Bill Holliday. "I say, Goodings, that is pretty shoddy language for an Englishman."

"Excuse me, Holliday. Soiled linen, gentlemen. Please get your soiled linen out here now."

~

One very devout layman was Doctor Robert Gardiner of the Montreal General Hospital who, along with his team there, pulled me through a living hell. They were truly instruments of grace and healing. When the surgeon gave me his final consultation and remarked that what was left of my leg was healing very well, he said, "You don't know how much I prayed for you, Bill." I cried. You just don't hear that sort of kindness every day, but it is there in people's hearts.

~

To the Roman Catholic clergy who befriended me, I am truly grateful. That friendship has lasted many years. How can I mention them all? Bishop Leonard Crowley supported us when he was at St. Patrick's Church twenty-five years ago. I valued my relationships with the Fathers Tom MacEntee, Brian Martin, Joe Sullivan and Murray McCrory. Emmett John (Pops) is retired but still active. Then there are Monseignors Matt Dube, Russell Breen, Neil Willard, Mgr. LeCavalier and my pal, Père Jacques Guilbault.

Wonderful friends in the United Church were the Reverends Ralph Watson, Dennis Dwyer and Bill Jay, while on the

Presbyterian side my special connections were the Reverends James Armour and John Simms.

The Armed Forces chaplains who shared with me are well remembered and their friendship is still much appreciated.

~

So it was that the Spirit of Christ followed me everywhere. When I was sinking, someone always came and lifted me up. Good people. God's people. Churchmen and women, doctors, policemen, storekeepers, accountants, artists, cartoonists, reporters, judges and lawyers. The staff of the Mission for over thirty-five years. But most of all, just ordinary nice people.

Do you remember the parable of the Good Samaritan? Well, you will recall that there was a priest who passed by on the other side, ignoring that person in need. Deep within me was the desire never to be that priest, but to do something and to be proud of what I did. From my boyhood on, that desire was fostered and fed by my church. It provided me with the professional tools to do the job and for that I am forever truly grateful.

Good intentions would never have been enough. Prayer, training and tradition kept me active and alive to what was happening. Knowing that the support was there allowed us to meet and defeat many challenges. Looking back at the traumatic sickness I fought for three bad years, I remember all the letters, visits and prayers I received while in hospital and during my convalescence and rehabilitation. They carried me through some very dark and terrifying times. Friends were there in great numbers. I felt the strength of their prayers and the love of my blessed Lord. They all helped me to accept a way of life that I had taught for over thirty years: one day at a time.

Martin Conroy was a great supporter of many of life's less favoured people. On the day that he was being celebrated as Montreal's Irishman of the Year, we came face to face in our wheelchairs. Martin was dying of bone cancer and had only a month more to live. I was close to tears as I said, "What can I say, Marty? Old Sir Harry Lauder said it best: "Keep right on to the end of the road."

Marty replied, "That's all we can do, Rev. God bless."

Finally, I shall never forget the address by Michael Ramsay, the 100th Archbishop of Canterbury, to the clergy of our Diocese many years ago. He said, "Wherever you go, you go to bring Christ to His people. When you get there, you will find that he is already there."

To which I can only add, "Alleluia."

~

May God be with you. `*Til we meet again.*

The Rev receiving The Order of Canada from
Governor General Jeanne Sauvé.

I expect to pass through this world but once.
any good that I may do,
let me do it now.
Let me not defer nor neglect it,
for I shall not pass this way again.

From an R.A.F. Service Book
Author Unknown

Printed in March 1996 by

VEILLEUX
ON DEMAND PRINTING INC.

in Boucherville, Quebec